MANCHESTER UNITED
Thirty Memorable Games
from the Fifties

IAIN McCARTNEY

MANCHESTER UNITED
Thirty Memorable Games
from the Fifties

First published in Great Britain in 2010 by
The Derby Books Publishing Company Limited, 3 The Parker
Centre, Derby, DE21 4SZ.

ISBN 978-1-85983-869-3

Printed and bound by Rzeszowskie Zakłady Graficzne S.A., Poland.

Contents

INTRODUCTION

Football in the 1950s was a far cry from the game that we are familiar with today.

For many, Saturday morning meant putting in a shift at work, with the sound of the 12 o'clock hooters signalling a mad dash for the exit, an even quicker bite to eat and then off to the match.

Stadiums were spartan, with little covered accommodation and terracing packed with swaying bodies eager to see the heroes of that period. Players, who had often travelled to the game on the same public transport as those supporters, frequently had another form of employment in order to supplement the meagre wages paid by their clubs.

Grass on the pitch after October was something of a rarity, with the muddy conditions doing little to create the perfect surface for the players, already handicapped with their ankle-high leather boots, heavy playing kit and even heavier match ball, on which to display their undoubted talents.

They did, however, entertain the masses who flocked to grounds on a weekly basis, conjuring up memories that lasted a lifetime. Games were written into the history of the clubs with incidents, and indeed complete 90 minutes, being narrated from father to son as the tradition of supporting a particular club was handed down through the generations.

The 1950s brought mixed fortunes for Manchester United. It was a decade that saw manager Matt Busby having to rebuild the team in the immediate post-war period and his assistant, Jimmy Murphy, forced into hauling the club back from the brink of despair and total collapse following the Munich air disaster.

The pages that follow take you back to those halcyon days of yesteryear, bringing to life those thrilling encounters and recalling the exploits of players who were to become legends in the history of Manchester United Football Club.

No. 1
UNITED V ASTON VILLA
8 March 1950

Having taken over as manager of Manchester United in February 1945, Matt Busby wasted little time in turning the players at his disposal into a regimented unit, capable of not simply winning games but of doing so in style. His former club, Liverpool, snatched the 1946–47 First Division title by one point, leaving the former Manchester City wing-half with the consolation of the runners'-up spot, something that he had to again be content with in the two campaigns that followed.

Lifting the FA Cup at Wembley Stadium in 1948, defeating Blackpool 4–2 in a still-talked-about Final, was certainly welcome compensation as the lust for the First Division title grew, but it was the Championship crown that the genial but totally focused Scot had set his eyes upon, determined to bring it to Old Trafford for the first time since season 1910–11.

Johnny Carey with the FA Cup after the 1948 Final win over Blackpool.

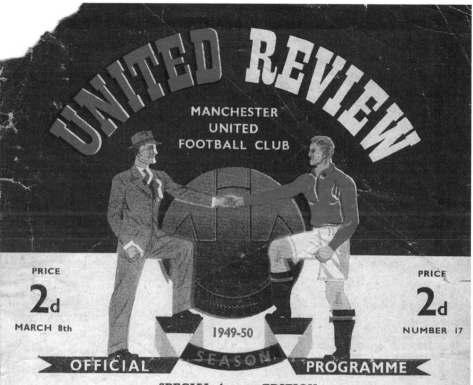

UNITED REVIEW

MANCHESTER
UNITED
FOOTBALL CLUB

PRICE

2d

MARCH 8th

1949-50

PRICE

2d

NUMBER 17

SEASON

OFFICIAL PROGRAMME

SPECIAL 4-page EDITION

WELCOME TO ASTON VILLA
BY TOM JACKSON
of the M/c Evening News

United's F.A. Cup story for 1949-50 is over following the 6th Round knock-out by Chelsea at Stamford Bridge, and so, once more, League affairs have to take pride of place.

This afternoon's visit of Aston Villa to Old Trafford, re-arranged because of Cup commitments, provides Matt Busby's men with a chance of improving their slender lead at the head of the First Division table.

Villa, who were without a fixture last weekend, went down 4—0 when United were at Villa Park last October. On that occasion they were without their Welsh international centre-forward, Trevor Ford, and the match opened with a remarkable goal in 45 seconds by Jack Rowley.

Strangely enough, Villa were runners-up on the two occasions United won the First Division championship—in 1908 and 1911. Thirty-nine years ago since top League honours came to Old Trafford—exactly the same interval which elapsed before United won the Cup for the second time in their history two years ago when, you will remember, they scored a great victory over Villa in the third round!

Despite their modest League position, Villa are capable of playing attractive football and can point to several outstanding personalities in their present ranks.

But, because of international calls imposed by the Wales v. Ireland clash this afternoon, neither Villa nor United will be able to field full-strength teams. Johnny Carey skippers Ireland and ex-Wigan Athletic full-back, Johnny Ball will probably deputise for him, while Villa will be without Trevor Ford, and centre-half Con Martin, who are on duty for Wales and Ireland respectively.

Last season, United ended a run of 18 successive League and Cup games without defeat by going down 2—1 at Villa Park, after accounting for Villa (3—1) in their home fixture at Maine Road.

When the clubs were in opposition at Villa Park last October, the teams were:—

United:—Crompton; Ball, Carey; Warner, Lynn, Cockburn; Delaney, Bogan, Rowley, Pearson and Mitten.

Villa:—Jones; Parkes, Dorsett; Powell, Martin, Moss (F.); Craddock, Dixon, Howarth, Lowe (E.), Goffin.

Scorers:—Rowley, Bogan, Mitten (2).

Season 1949–50 once again saw Busby's team challenging for that illusive title, and despite consecutive defeats against Burnley away and Sunderland at home, as September moved into October a run of nine unbeaten games leading up to early December kept them in a favourable position. As the campaign moved into its final couple of months, they had clawed their way to top spot, only fractionally ahead of arch-rivals Liverpool on goal difference.

Saturday 8 March saw Aston Villa travel north to Manchester, hoping to catch United in a rather subdued mood following their previous week's 2–0 FA Cup defeat at the hands of Chelsea, while the two clubs immediately behind them, Liverpool and Blackpool, faced each other at Anfield. Little did the Midland side know what lay in store for them amid the industrial sprawl of Trafford Park – had goalkeeper Joe Rutherford experienced any premonitions as to that afternoon's match then he certainly would not have made the journey north from Birmingham.

The opening minutes of the encounter were of little guide as to what lay in store, with the visitors putting United, and Johnny Carey in particular, playing in the totally unfamiliar position of centre-half, under pressure. United's captain was perhaps fortunate that Villa's regular number nine, Trevor Ford, was on international duty for Wales at Wrexham, as the powerfully built forward (who was to soon become the first player involved in a £30,000 transfer) would certainly have given Carey a difficult afternoon in the centre of the United defence. Con Martin, whose son Mick would in later years pull on the red shirt of Manchester United, was another notable Villa omission and another whose presence on this particular afternoon might well have made something of a difference to the scoreline.

John Aston put goalkeeper Jack Crompton, who had only returned to first-team duty a couple of weeks previously, under unnecessary pressure on more than one occasion with rather hurried back passes as Aston Villa attacked, but the United full-back was soon pushing forward at every opportunity in support of his front players. He did, however, breathe a sigh of relief when his rather untimely challenge on Smith, who had been sent clear by Powell, saw the referee point to the penalty spot and Goffin's rather feeble spot-kick was saved comfortably by the dependable Crompton.

Despite the visitors' constant back-pedalling and the home side's fluent, attacking football, such superiority could not be converted into goals, and in reality United should have been at least 3–0 in front by the interval. It was not until five minutes prior to the break that the deadlock was finally broken.

Jimmy Delaney, looking more like his old self on the United right after a few, rather uncharacteristic, disappointing displays, moved dangerously into the Villa penalty area, but as he went to go past Amos Moss, the younger, less experienced of the Moss brothers in the Aston Villa half-back line, the defender tripped him up, and referee R. S. Lloyd had no hesitation in once again pointing to the penalty spot. Charlie Mitten stepped up and made no mistake with the resulting kick.

If United's superior first-half football was not reflected in the actual scoreline as the teams left the pitch at half-time, those who delayed their return from seeking refreshments or relief at the primitive toilets of the time missed Busby's team turn their undoubted superiority into goals. Within three minutes of the referee's whistle restarting the game, United were three in front.

Charlie Mitten.

A foul on Downie, with Frank Moss the offender on this occasion, gave Mitten the opportunity to score a second from the penalty spot, and within minutes he had claimed his hat-trick, heading home a Jack Rowley cross.

Villa, to their credit, continued in their attempt to get a foothold on the game with Powell, their right half-back, putting in a fine afternoon's work. It was to be for little reward, though, as well as little concern for the home defence, and with the play regularly confined to one half of the pitch United were soon to increase their lead.

With 22 minutes of the second half played, Jack Rowley made it 4–0, evading a rather hopeful challenge from Amos Moss before giving Rutherford in the Villa goal little chance with a powerful right-footed drive – a goal typical of the United centre-forward.

Two minutes later a Delaney shot was headed clear by the younger of the Moss brothers, but only as far as Johnny Downie, who wasted little time in returning it in the direction from which it had come for United's fifth. The same player could quite easily have made it 6–0 as United regained possession straight from the restart, but this time the inside-right's effort cannoned off the Villa crossbar and away to safety.

Villa were now little match for a rampant United, although Gibson and Dixon tried their best to cause the United defence some problems, but they were to receive little change from half-backs Jack Warner and Henry Cockburn.

It was the attacking play of United that received most of the applause from the rather sparsely filled Old Trafford. With the official attendance given as 22,149, it was some 31,779 fewer than the highest attendance recorded at the ground that season. Those who had given the game a miss, for whatever reason, would rue their decision when they learnt of the result in the Saturday evening newspapers.

A sixth goal did eventually come, through Downie in the 77th minute, with the inside-forward finishing off a superb Delaney-Mitten move, although most of the United team seemed to be involved at some point or other. The visitors would certainly not have complained had the referee blown for full time there and then instead of restarting the game, as even hopes of a consolation goal looked totally unlikely.

Unfortunately, Villa were subjected to further United attacks and an inevitable seventh goal, with Charlie Mitten claiming his fourth of the afternoon and a hat-trick of penalties two minutes from time. The United outside-left once again repeated what he had done with the previous two spot-kicks, sending them low and hard into the bottom left-hand corner, giving the 'keeper no chance whatsoever.

Had United managed to notch double figures against Villa, it would not have been a total surprise to those present, such was their overall performance, but looking back one wonders what might have happened had Goffin converted that penalty-kick for Villa early in the game.

Reflecting on those United penalty awards, there was certainly nothing malicious regarding any of the challenges, but the referee viewed the moves from the Villa defenders that sent the United attackers sprawling as denying a scoring opportunity and was certainly justified in pointing to the spot.

Charlie Mitten's hat-trick of penalties, although something of rare event, had occurred previously, with Turnbull of Hibs having already done it this season and Milburn of Chesterfield having done likewise in 1947. Others to add their name to the feat were Barton of Sheffield United, playing as a guest for Rotherham in 1944, Walker of Aston Villa in 1921 and Horne of Lincoln City in 1935.

Through the passage of time, a story circulated that Mitten rather cheekily told Rutherford to what side of the goal he was going to place the ball prior to each kick. When asked many years later, the United inside-forward smiled and said, 'I didn't the first time, just in case he thought it was a fluke, but yes, I did tell him where I was going to put the next two.'

Despite that seven-goal victory over Aston Villa, which gave United a two-point advantage over second-place Liverpool, hopes of landing the First Division title were to soon evaporate. A 3–2 win at Middlesbrough three days later kept things on course, as did a goalless draw at home to Liverpool on 15 March, but Matt Busby could only sit and watch his hopes of the title disappear into thin air.

Blackpool won 2–1 at Old Trafford, and the following Saturday brought United a 3–1 defeat at Huddersfield. Three points from the first four games in April was certainly not Championship form, but, with three games to play, the name of Manchester United was still above the rest in the First Division League table.

The 2–0 defeat at home to Portsmouth, followed by a 2–1 defeat at Newcastle, brought an end to any title hopes, and the final-day 3–0 victory over Fulham at home simply earned United fourth spot, leaving the slump and decline to be debated in pubs, on public transport and in countless homes across the country for the next few weeks.

In those final 10 games of the season, the United goal machine of Charlie Mitten, Stan Pearson, Jack Rowley and company failed to find the net on four occasions and scored a mere eight goals. Three of those came on that final day when Fulham visited Old Trafford.

Would Busby be able to convert his Cup winners into First Division champions? Only time would tell.

Manchester United: Crompton, Ball, Aston, Warner, Carey, Cockburn, Delaney, Downie, Rowley, Pearson, Mitten.
Scorers: Mitten 4 (3 penalties), Downie 2, Rowley.
Aston Villa: Rutherford, Parkes, Dorsett, Powell, A. Moss, F. Moss, Dixon, Gibson, J. Harrison, Goffin, L. Smith.
Attendance: 22,149.

No. 2
UNITED V SUNDERLAND
26 December 1950

Compared to the first three seasons of the immediate post-war years, season 1949–50 had brought something of a disappointment for United as they could only finish in fourth place. It was hoped that some improvement could be achieved in the 1950–51 campaign, with a return to the form that took them to within touching distance of that illusive First Division Championship.

The season, however, started in a similar vein to how 1949–50 had finished, with only one win in three games. Although Fulham were beaten 1–0 in the opening fixture at Old Trafford, the two away matches that followed at Anfield and Burnden Park both brought defeats, 2–1 at Liverpool and by the only goal of the game at Bolton.

Liverpool then travelled along the East Lancs Road and were beaten 1–0, with Blackpool's visit to Manchester ending the same way. The away fixture at Villa Park saw United win 3–1, a

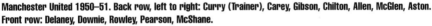

Manchester United 1950–51. Back row, left to right: Curry (Trainer), Carey, Gibson, Chilton, Allen, McGlen, Aston. Front row: Delaney, Downie, Rowley, Pearson, McShane.

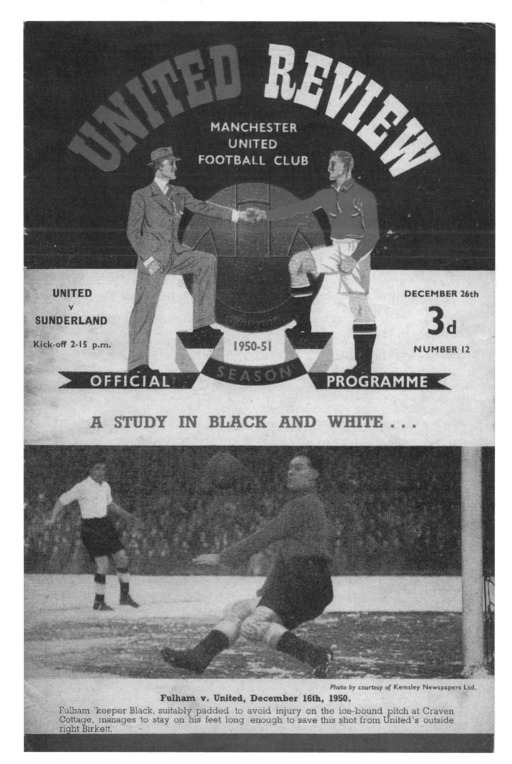

Fulham v. United, December 16th, 1950.

Fulham 'keeper Black, suitably padded to avoid injury on the ice-bound pitch at Craven Cottage, manages to stay on his feet long enough to save this shot from United's outside right Birkett.

result that left United only two points behind early leaders Arsenal. Instead of building on this, the inconsistency again set in, with two games without either a win or a goal followed by only one point being dropped in the next four outings. And so it continued until the end of the year.

The Christmas period can be an opportunity to make up lost ground, with a flurry of fixtures, but the Yuletide of 1950 proved to be United's worst for 17 years.

'Fantasy, worthy of Walt Disney's pictorial genius, took over the match between Manchester United and Sunderland at Old Trafford yesterday, and after a riot in which eight goals were scored, one had to record that Sunderland were victors by five goals to three,' wrote the *Manchester Guardian's* 'Old International', the incomparable Don Davies, but was he simply using his pen to create a more spectacular picture than what was actually played out on the worn Old Trafford pitch?

The pitch certainly was worn, as George Follows of the *Daily Herald*, another of the scribes from the newspapers of the day, who was in attendance at the game, wrote that it was 'a treacherous pig of a pitch'.

It is not often that United concede five goals, never mind at Old Trafford, but on Boxing Day 1950 Sunderland exploited the frailties in the home defence, caused, in the opinions of many, by Matt Busby's ongoing decision to play John Aston at centre-forward.

Aston, a member of the 1948 FA Cup-winning side and the regular left-back since March 1947, a position in which he won England international honours, found himself thrown into the fray as a stand-in centre-forward, having replaced Stan Pearson only a couple of weeks previously at Leeds Road, Huddersfield, on 9 December, where he scored twice in the 3–2 win. Further goals against Bolton at home and Sunderland away saw him retain his place, with Pearson himself having to be content in taking over the number-11 shirt.

Aston's performances were of such a standard that he was named the *News Chronicle* Player of the Month for December, and he also gained further England honours as a centre-forward.

Goals had certainly been leaked – 11 in the previous five games – so the punters most definitely had a point as there was really no way that United, who at the time were within touching distance of the leaders, should have conceded five to a team six places from the bottom of the First Division. Having said that, the visit to Roker Park on Christmas Day saw a second consecutive defeat, with the home side winning 2–1.

Just 24 hours later the two teams again came face to face, this time at at Old Trafford, having most likely made the journey down from the North East together following the Roker Park fixture. Busby had made a couple of changes to his Christmas Day selection, bringing in Bogan at inside-left and McShane at outside-right, and as the game got under way it looked as if the new-look forward line was going to bring something of a change in fortunes.

With only three minutes gone, Aston, looking everything a centre-forward should, crafted an opening for Bogan down the right before moving towards the Sunderland penalty area, taking up the perfect position to receive Bogan's cross and steered the ball wide of Mapson in the Sunderland goal for United's opener.

It was a lead that they managed to hold for no more than 60 seconds, mainly due to a dreadful error by Reg Allen. A long ball forward saw the United 'keeper advance from his goal to gather a lob from Tommy Wright, but he somehow managed to misjudge the bounce of the ball and it flew over his head, presenting Billy Bingham with an open goal into which to pop the equaliser.

With luck not having been exactly in great evidence in the past few weeks, it was a feeling of 'here we go again' for many, and this was further enhanced when Walsh, clearly in an offside position, was played on by a fortunate deflection off a United defender, allowing him the opportunity to have a shot at goal. His effort beat Allen but rattled off the crossbar; however, it landed at the feet of Broadis, who put Sunderland 3–1 in front.

Broadis, at ease on the hard, frozen surface, added his second and Sunderland's fourth before the groans from the United support had subsided, and within 14 minutes he had completed his hat-trick following an end-to-end move after an incident in the Sunderland goalmouth.

With the ball in his arms, having stopped a United attack, Mapson was caught by Aston and was sent reeling, with the United forwards claiming that the loose ball had crossed the goalline. Amid the shouts, with the referee turning a deaf ear, the ball was swiftly dispatched towards the United goal. Once again the ball bobbled precariously near the goalline, but it appeared that a defender managed to keep it out. He only succeeded in diverting it towards the waiting Broadis, though, who accepted the opportunity to claim his hat-trick.

In between Broadis scoring his second and third, Aston had furthered his cause with his second of the game, drifting past two defenders before his shot hit Mapson on the knees, then bounced off Bogan's chest to the makeshift centre-forward.

If there was any Christmas goodwill then it was United who were showing it to their guests, although, to be fair, they did create a couple of opportunities that may have brought goals. Rowley, who also missed a penalty, shooting straight at the Sunderland 'keeper, came close with one effort, while a Bogan shot skimmed the crossbar. By the time Bogan turned a bungled clearance by the Sunderland goalkeeper over the line for United's third, the game was well out of their reach as the Roker Park side had scored their fifth.

Broadis again was at the thick of things, flicking the ball through towards Davis for what Don Davies considered 'the gift of the season', allowing the centre-forward to convert the opportunity with ease. A sixth could easily have followed, but McGlen spared the blushes of Chilton by preventing a certain own-goal.

The Old Trafford crowd began to head for the exit gates long before the end, looking forward to the left-over turkey more than the final whistle, but they would be back in a matter of days for the visit of Oldham Athletic in the FA Cup.

The Cup gave United some breathing space and, admittedly against lesser opposition, they scored four in each of the opening two rounds. This also gave the team some much-needed confidence, and, although John Aston continued in his centre-forward role, the defence became more solid and reliable,

The first League game of the New Year saw Tottenham Hotspur beaten 2–1 on 13 January, and it wasn't until 7 April and the away fixture at Stoke City that United experienced their first League defeat of 1951. They had by then lost 1–0 to Birmingham City in the FA Cup.

By the beginning of March, United's consistency had seen them climb to third place in the First Division, five points behind leaders Tottenham, and by 14 April they were second, now

Allenby Chilton.

only four points behind the London club, who had lost 2–0 to Huddersfield Town that same afternoon, with three games remaining.

Newcastle United were beaten 2–0, Huddersfield Town were trounced 6–0, and on the final Saturday of the season Blackpool held them to a 1–1 draw at Bloomfield Road. Tottenham, however, matched them every step of the way and lifted the title with a four-point cushion.

Had it not been for the failure to win at home between 7 October and 13 January, and most certainly the two consecutive defeats against Sunderland, then the Championship trophy would more than likely have resided at Old Trafford 12 months earlier than it actually did. The transfer of Jimmy Delaney to Aberdeen in November, when he was still a first-team regular, left something of a void and a position that Matt Busby failed to fill until the acquisition of Johnny Berry almost a year later.

But what of the United supporters of the time? How did they feel? Among the page full of letters in the *News Chronicle* for Tuesday 16 January 1951, most were full of praise for Busby's vision in moving Aston to centre-forward, but they were also quick with their comments that the defence was much more fragile without his presence.

'To criticise United any other way than constructively after four seasons of the highest-class and most entertaining football would be ungracious,' wrote H.B. Taylor of Northenden. 'They are passing through a period of transition, but we shall be hearing from them again shortly, when the correct blend has been achieved.

'What a find Aston is at centre-forward. Unfortunately, the goals against show he is missed in defence and Matt Busby must have a first-class headache wishing for Johnny Aston twins to use both in attack and defence.'

There was, however, one issue that brought overwhelming praise, and that was the investment in youth, which would undoubtedly bring success in the future, as S. Bennett of Newton Heath was to prophesy: 'When the Matt Busby school for football finishes its term and pupils Birkett, Birch, McNulty and Jones are passed out fully-trained craftsmen, then we shall see a great United again.'

There was also a positive side to the defeats by the Wearsiders, as it seemed to transform United from an inconsistent 11 to a team that had the confidence and belief in itself to overcome the poor start to the campaign and the previously mentioned shortcomings. They were to lose only nine First Division games in the next 59 as they strode to their first post-war Championship in 1951–52.

Manchester United: Allen, Carey, McGlen, Gibson, Chilton, Cockburn, McShane, Bogan, Aston, Pearson, Rowley.
Scorers: Bogan 2, Aston.
Sunderland: Mapson, Hedley, Hudgell, McLean, Walsh, A. Wright, Bingham, T. Wright, Davis, Brodis, Watson.
Scorers: Broadis 3, Bingham, Davis.
Attendance: 35,176.

No. 3
UNITED V ARSENAL
26 April 1952

If the modern-day United supporter thought that 26 years was a long time to wait for the chance to see their favourites lift the First Division Championship trophy, imagine how their pre-war counterparts felt.

Having gained entry, as Newton Heath, to the First Division in 1892, their inexperience, coupled with poor form, saw them relegated via the end-of-season Test matches in 1894, having finished 16th in both of their two seasons in the top flight.

Despite a name change to Manchester United in 1902 there was no change in fortune, as it took 12 seasons to regain their place among the elite clubs in the land, and even then it was as runners-up. Life as a United supporter in those distant days was often as dismal as the surroundings where they were forced to watch their football.

Back in the First Division, under the expert guidance of Ernest Mangnall, the team, which included the likes of Charlie Roberts and the former Manchester City favourite Billy Meredith, suddenly discovered a fine vein of form, and, after finishing eighth in 1906–07, the name of Manchester United was engraved on a League Championship trophy for the first time 12 months later.

Season 1908–09 saw United drop to 13th, but the blow was softened by the club's first FA Cup victory, which was followed, thanks mainly to the goals of Sandy Turnbull and George Wall, by a second First Division title two years later. Aside from that, United's fortunes plummeted, and the team were fortunate not to make the drop down to the Third Division in 1933–34, when a last-gasp win at Millwall secured their safety.

The arrival of Matt Busby brought a distinct change in fortune, although finishing second for three consecutive seasons between 1946–47 and 1948–49 and then fourth in 1949–50 cast up doubts as to whether the 29-year jinx, not including the 11 wartime seasons, would ever be broken. The Second Division was won in 1935–36 and the Football League Northern Section, Second Championship in 1941–42, but it was the First Division Championship that really mattered.

As season 1951–52 got under way, with three wins and a draw and 13 goals scored in the process, hopes were high for a favourable campaign. A 1–0 defeat at Bolton appeared to be something of a minor blip, as three victories and a draw got the show back on the road, although this was followed by two consecutive defeats, against Tottenham 2–0 at White Hart Lane, and 2–1 against Preston North End at Old Trafford.

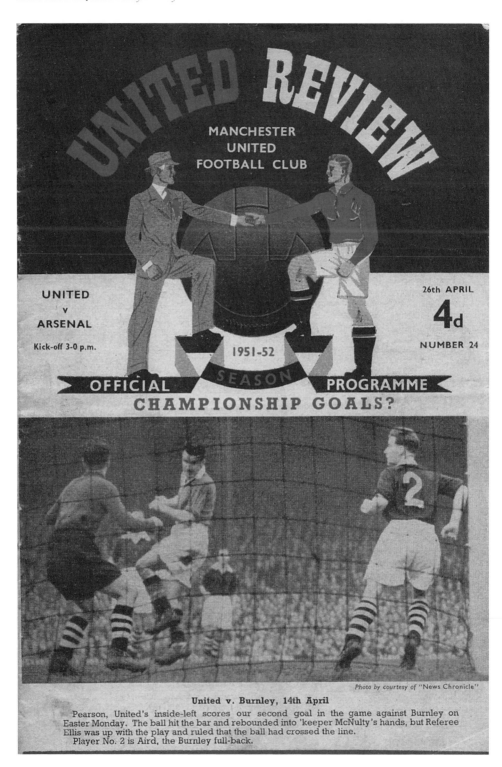

UNITED REVIEW

MANCHESTER
UNITED
FOOTBALL CLUB

UNITED
v
ARSENAL

Kick-off 3-0 p.m.

26th APRIL

4d

NUMBER 24

1951-52

SEASON

OFFICIAL PROGRAMME

CHAMPIONSHIP GOALS?

Photo by courtesy of "News Chronicle"

United v. Burnley, 14th April

Pearson, United's inside-left scores our second goal in the game against Burnley on Easter Monday. The ball hit the bar and rebounded into 'keeper McNulty's hands, but Referee Ellis was up with the play and ruled that the ball had crossed the line.

Player No. 2 is Aird, the Burnley full-back.

The late autumn form suddenly became a cause for concern, as only three of the following eight fixtures were won, and many began to think that it was going to be yet another season among the also-rans, as the 0–0 draw at Anfield on 24 November saw them occupy seventh place in the First Division table, five points behind leaders Portsmouth.

Two months later, having made an early FA Cup third-round exit at the hands of Hull City in front of a disheartened 43,517 at Old Trafford, the disappointment was softened slightly by the sight of the name 'Manchester United' sitting at the top of the First Division table, albeit on goal difference above Pompey, following the 2–0 home victory over Tottenham Hotspur.

By the beginning of March United were still in the top spot, but consecutive defeats, 3–2 at Huddersfield Town and 1–0 at Portsmouth, had allowed Arsenal to make up the difference in points and the two sides were now level. Burnley then held them to a 1–1 draw at Turf Moor on Good Friday, and the pressure was now looking as though it was beginning to take its toll.

Twenty-four hours later Liverpool arrived at Old Trafford but were sent home along the East Lancs Road on the back of a 4–0 defeat, with the *Sunday Express* proclaiming that 'Top-gear United had Championship look'. There were now only four games remaining, but Arsenal were still perched on United's shoulder awaiting a slip, although a 2–1 defeat at Bolton (their first since 29 December) on the back of their FA Cup semi-final victory over Chelsea gave United a slight advantage.

Two days after the trouncing of Liverpool, Burnley visited Old Trafford, but any fears of the Turf Moor side throwing a spanner in the works never materialised, as Roger Byrne switched from left-back to outside-left in a Matt Busby master-stroke. He scored twice, making it five in three games, as United signalled their Championship intentions with an emphatic 6–1 win.

Arsenal clawed it back to only goal difference with a victory over Stoke, as United could only manage a point at Bloomfield Road against Blackpool. Much was, therefore, to lie on the results of the penultimate fixture of the 1951–52 season on Monday 21 April, when Chelsea travelled north to Old Trafford and Arsenal travelled to The Hawthorns to face West Bromwich Albion.

Sensing that the Championship was theirs for the taking, United overwhelmed their visitors, winning 3–0, only prevented from a fourth by a Byrne penalty miss. Arsenal, on the other hand, returned south on the end of a 3–1 defeat.

That should have been it then, as United would now be two points in front of the Gunners and they had a superior goal difference. However, by a strange quirk of fate, the fixtures for the 1951–52 season had thrown United and Arsenal together at Old Trafford on the final day of the campaign and, although highly unlikely, if the visitors returned to London with a seven-goal victory then they were champions. Having only made the return journey south with just one point since the resumption of League football since World War Two, it looked highly unlikely.

Arsenal had actually conceded the title that previous Monday, following their defeat at the Hawthorns, with both manager Tom Whittaker and captain Joe Mercer sending telegrams to Old Trafford which read: 'All at Arsenal send you congratulations on a worthy Championship win.'

Such was the occasion at Old Trafford on that final day of the season, it was little wonder that the gates were locked some 15 minutes before kick-off with a crowd just short of the 55,000 capacity inside. Despite the chances of the Gunners actually scoring anywhere near seven being rather remote, a few thousand had made their way to Manchester from London, clinging to a slender thread of hope.

Kicking off, heading towards the Stretford End, United were soon on the attack. Byrne, clearly relishing his new-found lease of life on the left wing, quickly stepped into the action, and within eight minutes of the start any hopes that Arsenal and their followers had of snatching the Championship were thrown to the wind as United took the lead. Johnny Carey lobbed the ball into the visitors' goalmouth, where Stan Pearson rose to head it backwards to the feet of Jack Rowley, who fired home.

It could quite easily have been Arsenal who had taken the lead, but after having dribbled the ball some 40 yards down the left wing, Roper's long ball into the United area went behind before Cox could get to it.

Moments after having taken the lead, the crowd were again screaming 'Goal!' Rowley gathered a deflected shot from Carey and his strike cannoned off the underside of Swindin's crossbar and bounced precariously on the goalline. Appeals were made that the ball had actually bounced behind the line, but the referee waved play on and the ball ended up being kicked into the side netting.

Johnny Berry.

United were soon well in command of the play, and Rowley once again came close to adding to that solitary goal lead, but on this occasion it was the head of Shaw, the Arsenal centre-half, that got in the way. A Pearson through ball gave Downie the opportunity to move towards goal, but before he could manage a shot he was fouled by Mercer, who was spoken to by the referee. The resulting free-kick was cleared but, regaining possession, Rowley beat Shaw. His shot flew across the face of the Arsenal goal, though, and went inches wide of the post. It was surely just a matter of time before United would get that second goal.

A Byrne centre was headed clear by Smith, while at the opposite end Chilton completely mis-kicked and Holton seized possession before slipping the ball to Cox. Creating space for himself, the Gunners' right-winger had the ideal opportunity to score, but his shot went well wide of the target and almost hit the corner flag.

With United faltering slightly, Holton outpaced Chilton and shot for goal as Reg Allen came out to narrow the angle, the 'keeper doing his job correctly, and the ball bulged into the side netting. The United custodian was beaten soon afterwards, although he was relieved to see the shot from Cox flash past the wrong side of the post.

It wasn't until five minutes before the interval that the second goal came. Forbes, the Arsenal right-half, took a knock as he moved forward in support of his teammates and was lying injured as the ball was quickly moved forward and back towards the visitors' goal. Pearson gained possession, and his shot seemed to take a deflection off Mercer as it flew past the stranded Swindin and into the net.

Two minutes later it was 3–0. Rowley was given the ball on the byline, midway between the corner flag and the Arsenal goal, and through sheer determination dribbled past one white-shirted defender, then another, and as Swindin moved forward to block his route to goal the United centre-forward unselfishly pushed the ball back to Byrne, who had nothing more to do than side-foot the ball into an unguarded net.

A suspected fractured wrist kept Shaw, who was injured in the 22nd minute, in the visitors' dressing room as the second half got under way, but despite being reduced to 10 men it was Arsenal who enjoyed the best of the play in the opening minutes, with a shot from Roper going narrowly wide. United soon regained their poise, though, and created the need for a double save from Swindin, beating down a Byrne centre before grasping the ball as both Rowley and Cockburn moved in.

Play continued to move from end to end, with both goalkeepers doing well to keep the ball out. Swindin, partly unsighted in a crowded goalmouth, did well to save an Aston shot, while at the opposite end Allen had to come racing out of his penalty area to boot the ball clear.

Downie, from a Byrne centre, and Rowley both had the ball in the net, but on each occasion the linesman's flag went up for offside. The standard of play had by now slowly deteriorated, with both Berry and Carey spurning good goal-scoring opportunities.

The crowd were brought back to life in the 74th minute when Rowley scored United's fourth. Carey lobbed the ball down the middle, and the United centre-forward raced through on goal. As Swindin raced from his net, Rowley calmly lifted the ball over the advancing 'keeper's head to score.

Two minutes later there was a fifth goal, but this time it was for Arsenal, Cox beating Allen from close in after Holton had created the opening. The goal brought polite applause from the home support.

With eight minutes still to play, United showed no signs of letting up, and with the ball once again in the Arsenal penalty area the referee stopped the game and pointed to the penalty spot before speaking to several of the Arsenal players. From the spot-kick Jack Rowley completed his hat-trick with what was his record 30th goal of the season, bending back the wrists of the Arsenal 'keeper as he tried in vain to stop the ball.

Shaw had failed to return to the field, but until now the visitors had coped admirably. Their ranks, however, were depleted further for the final four minutes when Roper was forced to leave the pitch and, with a minute remaining, the nine men conceded a sixth goal, Man of the Match Rowley setting up Stan Pearson, who slammed the ball home.

As the final whistle blew there was an enthusiastic pitch invasion by a vast number of supporters, both young and old, and amid the confusion and chaos the Beswick Prize Band struck up *See the Conquering Heroes Come*, which was obviously note perfect as they had been practising it now for a considerable number of years! As the players struggled through the throngs of supporters, the band rounded off with *Auld Lang Syne* before being almost trampled underfoot.

'We want Carey,' shouted the crowd congregated around the mouth of the tunnel, but they were to be disappointed as neither the United captain nor any of his teammates appeared. They then drifted off in the direction of the station, to the long line of buses on Chester Road or simply to the nearest pub to celebrate United's first post-war Championship success. The United players, having scrubbed and changed, were later to make their way to Manchester Town Hall, where the Lord Mayor held a civic reception in their honour.

Manchester United: Allen, McNulty, Aston, Carey, Chilton, Cockburn, Berry, Downie, Rowley, Pearson, Byrne.
Scorers: Rowley 3, Pearson 2, Byrne.
Arsenal: Swindin, Barnes, Smith, Forbes, Shaw, Mercer, Cox, Goring, Holton, Lewis, Roper.
Scorer: Cox.
Attendance: 53,651

No. 4

WALTHAMSTOW AVENUE V UNITED

31 January 1953 and 5 February 1953

Everybody loves a winner, especially if they come out on top against the odds, gaining the upper hand over someone much bigger and stronger. Giant killing in the FA Cup certainly falls into both of those categories.

As the black, numbered balls rattle around in the maroon velvet bag, the big boys of the Football League always want a home draw, and if they are paired with one of the minnows form the lower regions then all the better. The embarrassment of being drawn against a team that they rarely come up against, on some small nondescript ground, and being dumped out of the world's number-one knock-out competition does not bear thinking about.

When the draw was made for the fourth round of the 1953 FA Cup competition and the amateurs of Walthamstow Avenue followed Manchester United out of the bag, there was a massive sigh of relief around Old Trafford. Few gave the FA Amateur Cup holders any chance of inflicting a Cup upset.

It was the first time in 24 years that a club of amateur status had reached this stage of the competition, and Walthamstow secretary Mr Jim Lewis said, 'The draw could not have been much better, and we may as well play against the best side. If we win at Old Trafford we shall have proved ourselves. A tie nearer home – preferably at Arsenal – would have suited us better, but we shall still have plenty of support.'

Most, if not all, of the United supporters were confident of the win. One supporter, C.G. Massey of Levenshulme, was so certain that United would progress into round five that he wrote to the *Manchester Evening Chronicle* suggesting the club should be issuing vouchers to those who attended the Walthamstow Cup tie so that they would have priority when tickets went on sale.

This, however, was the Manchester United of the early 1950s and, despite winning the First Division Championship the previous season, it was a team on the wane and about to go through

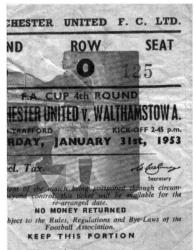

A ticket from the 1953 FA Cup fourth round.

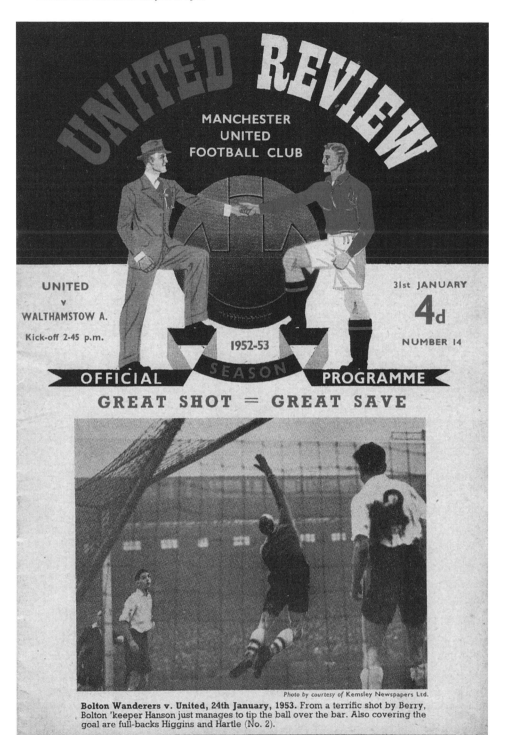

Bolton Wanderers v. United, 24th January, 1953. From a terrific shot by Berry, Bolton 'keeper Hanson just manages to tip the ball over the bar. Also covering the goal are full-backs Higgins and Hartle (No. 2).

Jack Rowley.

something of a transitional period. But surely Mr Massey was right and United would be progressing to round five?

Matt Busby was also confident: 'It could not have been a better draw for us. We fully respect these amateurs but do not expect to find them as difficult to dispose of as Millwall.' United had beaten the London side 1–0 in the previous round.

In more modern times the team would have been a completely different United side to the one that had played in the League fixture during the previous week, with Sir Alex Ferguson giving some of his squad players an opportunity to show that they were more than capable of playing on a more regular basis at a higher level. But in 1953 Matt Busby only made one change to the team that had lost 2–1 at Bolton seven days previously, replacing David Pegg with Jack Rowley.

Having travelled north with a few injury worries, the Walthamstow manager, although having selected his starting 11 some three days previously, left it until half an hour prior to kick-off before publicly naming his team. Those selected lined up to face United in what was undoubtedly the biggest game in the amateur club's history, something that was clearly highlighted with their travelling support of well over 1,000.

The amateurs carried out the first assault on goal, and it was only Chilton's quick intervention that stopped Lewis from having a clear run to the net, with the same player also being pulled up on two other occasions due to being caught in an offside position.

It was United, however, who claimed the first shot on goal. Chilton lobbed the ball forward into the Walthamstow goalmouth, where Rowley managed to get his head to it, nodding it down to Pearson, but his shot on the turn went inches wide. They also had the ball in the net after only nine minutes, when a Berry cross was gathered by Avenue 'keeper Gerula, who was then bundled rather unceremoniously over the line by United centre-forward Eddie Lewis. The referee judged it as an unfair challenge and ruled the goal out.

Walthamstow were certainly not overawed by the occasion, or if they were it didn't show in their play as they were strong in the tackle and quick on the break whenever possible, and although often penned back in their own half they showed plenty of defensive spirit, with Saunders, Young and Stratton standing firm as United continued to push forward in search of that breakthrough goal.

Chilton forced Gerula into making a fine save with a powerful drive from 50 yards away, which, assisted by the wind, flew towards the Walthamstow goal. Another attempt from 40 yards shortly afterwards was again brilliantly saved. The 'keeper also managed to keep his team in the game with other notable saves, including knocking clear a shot from Berry for a corner and again from the resulting flag kick. He punched away Carey's header for yet another corner. A goalmouth scramble ensued, but in the end Downie shot wide.

Ray Wood, on the other hand, was little more than a spectator, and it wasn't until about a minute before the break that he kicked the ball for the first time that afternoon.

As the interval approached the nerves of the home side began to tell. Rowley was spoken to by the referee for a foul on the 'keeper, but United seemed to regain their composure and for almost five minutes bombarded the visitors' goal. Aston, Chilton, Rowley and Pearson all tried their luck with shots, but somehow they all failed to reach their intended destination.

Downie then stumbled but managed to regain his footing and push the ball out wide to Berry. Without much hesitation the winger crossed the ball into the centre, and there was Eddie Lewis to head it into the far corner.

Facing the wind as the teams changed ends, United soon discovered that this would be an additional handicap for them to overcome when an early clearance by Stratton sailed the length of the Old Trafford pitch and into the arms of Wood.

Lewis should have made it 2–0 soon after the restart when he was put clean through by Downie, but he completely mis-kicked and the ball trickled goalwards and into the arms of Gerula. Pearson also missed a chance to increase the lead, his effort hitting the side netting. Rowley then struck the crossbar from a Berry cross.

Surprisingly, United were coping better against the wind than they had in the first half, when it was on their backs, but although in command they could not deliver the goods in front of goal, and it began to look as if the single goal was going to take them through into the next round. But with 15 minutes to go the majority of the Old Trafford was stunned into silence. A free-kick was awarded against Roger Byrne and was delivered into the rather crowded United area, but for some reason it was not cleared, and Lewis, the Walthamstow centre-forward, quickly drove it past Wood for the equaliser.

Desperation now set in. Lewis of United again should have done better after a Saunders mis-kick but took too long to control the ball, and in the dying seconds Carey centred and the ball was picked up by Pearson, who managed to get round a defender, but he only half-hit the ball, which was comfortably collected by the Polish-born Gerula.

The referee's whistle brought something of a mini pitch invasion as the delighted Walthamstow supporters rushed on to congratulate their heroes. And rightly so, as it was a day of football history, with the might of Manchester United, the current First Division champions, held by a team of amateurs.

Jim Lewis, the Walthamstow secretary, got his Cup tie nearer home and at Arsenal, his preferred venue, but it was certainly a game that he never once could have envisaged when the draw was originally made. Moving the fixture to the North London ground allowed more supporters to attend while also allowing the amateur side to gain financially. United, at least, were familiar with the Highbury venue, if not the opposition, but despite the feelings that they could not play so badly again, there were also the dreaded thoughts of those travelling south that a Cup giant-killing could be on the cards.

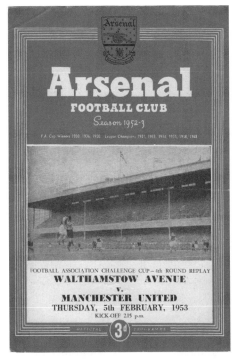

Arsenal
FOOTBALL CLUB
Season 1952-3

FOOTBALL ASSOCIATION CHALLENGE CUP — 4th ROUND REPLAY
WALTHAMSTOW AVENUE
v.
MANCHESTER UNITED
THURSDAY, 5th FEBRUARY, 1953
KICK-OFF 2.15 p.m.

Roger Byrne.

The actual decision to switch the tie from Walthamstow's compact 13,000-capacity stadium to Arsenal's Highbury home brought much controversy because they had refused to switch their earlier-round tie against Stockport County to White Hart Lane. Obviously they felt that they had a better chance of beating Stockport on their own ground and that United were a much bigger draw, enabling them to at least make some much-needed cash if they were not to progress any further in the competition.

The mid-week fixture attracted some 50,000 fans, and the majority of those were determined to be Walthamstow's 12th man, getting behind the amateurs from the start and assaulting United with a barrage of noise.

Lewis, the Avenue's centre-forward, once again caused the United defence and Chilton in particular countless problems, but after one narrow escape the visitors settled and hit Walthamstow with three quick goals, which in reality killed off any threat of a major Cup upset.

For the first, Rowley collected Carey's pass and moved away towards the right before centring the ball directly on to Pearson's head. The inside man made no mistake. Two minutes later Eddie Lewis controlled a Berry corner before giving Gerula little hope of stopping his low, hard drive. Before Walthamstow could recover, it was 3–0. Berry found Rowley, who calmly pulled Stratton out of position before shooting past the clutching fingers of the Avenue 'keeper.

Although clearly rattled, Walthamstow kept trying to break down the United defence, but a somewhat harshly awarded penalty was given for a foul on Pearson and was duly converted by Byrne. There was clearly no way back now.

Another rather dubious penalty award, this time to Walthamstow, almost on half-time, saw J. Lewis beat Wood and at least give his team some credibility, and then within minutes of the restart the same player had the crowd at fever pitch when he scored a second, heading the ball past a helpless Wood. For 15 minutes United were clearly on the ropes, with the Avenue rather unexpectedly back in the game.

Determined not to find themselves conceding further goals, United pushed forward as if they were in danger of going out of the competition, and Pearson, Berry and Rowley were all foiled by the superb Gerula. Such was their determination to add to their four goals, they almost conceded a third to the amateurs, with Bailey's effort going inches wide.

In the closing minutes United did add a fifth when Rowley scored with a long dropping shot from the left wing, which seemed to get caught in the wind and evade Gerula's outstretched fingers.

What United had done in the replay had been expected of them in the first game at Old Trafford, but credit had to be given to Walthamstow for taking their illustrious opponents to a replay. It is, however, fair to say that it was one man only who earned his team a replay and who kept the score down in the replay, and that was the 33-year-old Walthamstow 'keeper, Gerula, who had won international honours before coming to England.

Having breathed a big sight of relief, United were in round five, but it was to be as far as they would go as a visit to Goodison Park saw Everton progress into the quarter finals with a 2–1 victory.

Manchester United: Wood, Aston, Byrne, Carey, Chilton, Cockburn, Berry, Downie, Lewis, Pearson, Rowley.
Scorer: Lewis.
Walthamstow Avenue: S. Gerula, D. Young, L. Stratton, E. Harper, D. Saunders, D. Hall, T.E. Bailey, G. Lucas, J.L. Lewis, G. Fielder, K. Camis.
Scorer: J.L. Lewis.
Attendance: 34,748.

Replay
Manchester United: Wood, Aston, Byrne, Carey, Chilton, Cockburn, Berry, Lewis, Rowley, Pearson, Pegg.
Scorers: Rowley 2, Byrne (penalty), Lewis, Pearson.
Walthamstow Avenue: As above.
Scorer: J.L. Lewis 2.
Attendance: 49,119.

No. 5
UNITED V CARDIFF CITY
4 April 1953

On the morning of Friday 3 April 1953 a young 16-year-old United apprentice made his way nonchalantly down Warwick Road towards Old Trafford, where he would be employed sweeping the dressing rooms and terracing in preparation for the visit of Cardiff City, or helping clean boots or perhaps some other menial job afforded to the ground-staff youngsters.

Hands in his pockets, whistling the latest top tunes of the day and dreaming of the following afternoon's reserve-team fixture at Sheffield Wednesday's Hillsborough ground, he entered the red wooden door used by staff and players and made his way along underneath the main stand.

On that particular morning, however, the youngster didn't get too many of his usual chores done because he was rather surprisingly summoned to Matt Busby's office. As he made his way upstairs his mind was racing, wondering what he had done wrong and what the manager could possibly want him for.

Duncan Edwards (below), and as a school boy (above).

There was no hint of what the boss had called him for as the soft Scottish brogue said, 'Sit down, son.' The nervous apprentice was to remain silent for a few minutes longer as the manager suddenly told him, 'Go and get your boots, son, you're playing for the first team tomorrow against Cardiff City.'

Although obviously thrilled by the news, Duncan Edwards took it calmly, as he did most things, and after a brief chat with his manager he asked for permission to make a telephone call to his parents in the Black Country town of Dudley so that they could make their arrangements to travel to Manchester the following morning to watch their son make his Manchester United debut.

Photo by courtesy of the Provincial Press Agency, 88, Hart St., Southport

Back Row (left to right): Downie, Rowley, Aston, Allen, Chilton, Byrne, and Pearson.
Front Row (left to right): Berry, Carey, Cockburn, and McNulty. Trophies are the
F.A. Charity Shield (left), and the First Division Championship Cup (right).

Jackie Blanchflower.

David Pegg.

With the news broken and Edwards told that he didn't have to continue with his ground-staff duties – for that particular morning at least – he raced out of the ground, back over the Warwick Road railway bridge, across Chester Road, heading for his digs a couple of hundred yards further on in Birch Avenue, eager to tell his landlady, 'Ma' Watson, his news.

Mrs Watson, 'the best landlady anyone could wish for', was also 'mother' to the likes of Mark Jones, Jackie Blanchflower and David Pegg, who had all made their United debuts, so, although excited for Duncan, she took it all in her stride as she had done in the past with the others under her wing.

Within nine months of leaving school Duncan Edwards had made the Manchester United first team, having shone in the United Youth team as well as winning Lancashire FA recognition. He was no ordinary young footballing prospect; during his early days on the grass parks of Dudley and alongside his schoolboy friends he stood out as special.

Duncan's signing for United was like something out of a spy film, with Jimmy Murphy and Bert Whalley making the late-night journey from Manchester to Dudley and awakening the Edwards household in the early hours of 2 June 1952 in order to get the signature of the most sought-after youth in Britain. Seven days later the England Schoolboy star, along with another United signing, Gordon Clayton, waved goodbye to his parents at Dudley Station and headed for Manchester.

Season 1952–53 began with the tousle-haired prospect lining up in the pre-season public practice match for the junior Reds against the Blues, and he continued with appearances for the

United Colts in the Manchester Amateur League and for the A team. He had also made nine appearances in the Central League side, but it was in the FA Youth Cup that this precocious talent was suddenly thrust into the national spotlight.

Three days prior to his debut, George Follows, writing in the *News Chronicle* penned, 'Like the father of the first atom bomb, Manchester United are waiting for something tremendous to happen. This tremendous football force they have discovered in Duncan Edwards, who is exactly 16 and a half this morning.

'Though nobody can tell exactly what will happen when Edwards explodes into First Division football, one thing is certain: it will be spectacular.'

Follows continued to extol the virtues of the boy from the Priory Estate but finished his article, 'If you think this is a lot to write about a lad of 16, I can only say "You obviously haven't seen this boy Edwards."'

Duncan Edwards ran down the Old Trafford tunnel and out into the Easter sunshine for his United debut against a Cardiff City team that was situated mid-table in the First Division, some six points behind United. Fortunes throughout the season, as we have seen with the previously mentioned Cup encounters with Walthamstow Avenue, had been mixed, although the signing of Tommy Taylor from Barnsley, for a record £29,999, had brought about something of an improvement, with the Yorkshireman ending the season with seven goals from his 11 starts.

Don Gibson and Henry Cockburn had shared the left-half position for the majority of the season, but it was an injury to the latter that gave Duncan his opportunity. It was a debut perhaps like no other, as everyone with any interest in Manchester United was well aware of his undoubted ability and the expectations that those within the club held towards his future.

It was Cardiff's first appearance at Old Trafford since 13 October 1928, when they had shared the points in a 1–1 draw, and, like United, they were playing their second game in 48 hours, having been defeated 2–1 at Liverpool the previous day. United had been in London facing Charlton at The Valley, where they drew 2–2.

The debutant showed little in the way of nerves, and not only did he show his creative ability with some fine passes, he was also not shy when it came to having a shot at goal, with one early effort just flashing past the post.

Cardiff showed something of an aggressive streak, and Tommy Taylor found himself on the end of a rather forceful Montgomery tackle on the edge of the area as he moved forward, but the resulting free-kick from Rowley was well blocked.

Play quickly switched to the opposite end of the ground and another clumsy foul, this time by Chilton on Grant out by the touchline, was to prove fatal. Mansell centred the ball into the United area, where Chisholm rose to head it towards goal. Crompton, rather uncharacteristically, dropped the ball at the feet of Grant, and the Cardiff centre-forward gratefully accepted the gift. With only 11 minutes gone United were a goal behind.

Four minutes later they were 2–0 down. Cardiff pushed the ball down the middle, over the head of Chilton, and as the United centre-half chased after the ball Crompton raced from his line and dived on it. Somehow he failed to hold it, and it squirmed out of his grasp and rolled

Tommy Taylor.

favourably to Chisholm, who had nothing else to do except side-foot it into the unattended United net.

Two poor goalkeeping errors seemed to have an affect the whole United team. Following that second goal, countless passes went astray, although it had to be said that the young debutant was showing many of his older colleagues up with some of his play.

United attacks were few and far between, with the close-passing game proving costly on numerous occasions. Aston sent Berry scampering down the wing, and after beating a couple of players he attempted a one-two with Taylor, but the centre-forward's return ball was intercepted by Montgomery. Jack Rowley came the closest to pulling a goal back when he tried to take the ball round both a defender and the goalkeeper, but he took it too far and his shot went wide. Taylor then shot over from 25 yards.

United continued to live on tenterhooks and were rather fortunate not to go further behind when Crompton appeared to bring down Northcott as the Cardiff outside-left pushed the ball just wide of the post. There was silence around the ground as the referee consulted his linesman, who had raised his flag, but it was for nothing more than an offside decision against the Cardiff forward.

Howells saved well from Taylor, while Berry showed unusually poor finishing when set up by Pearson, but most of the first-half action was to be found around the United goal, where Edwards continued to perform well under pressure.

Within four minutes of the restart United should have reduced the arrears when Berry, having collected the ball from Gibson, sent in a low cross towards Pearson, who then laid the ball off to Rowley. The United inside-forward hurried his chance, however, when he could have taken more time, and the opportunity was gone.

United were clearly struggling, with their play often sluggish, and they were apt to hold onto the ball for too long, allowing Cardiff the opportunity to close them down. Trying to inject something into his team, Busby switched Taylor and Rowley but to little avail. The visitors, on the other hand, continued to impress, and on the hour mark they added a third.

Byrne should have cleared the ball out of defence but allowed Tiddy to dispossess him, and the Cardiff outside-right calmly pulled the ball back before hitting it towards goal. Crompton, standing in the middle of his net, was caught unaware and the ball bounced.

35

Even Edwards became affected by United's dismal performance and, like Byrne, was now being caught in possession. In one instance Williams clawed the ball from the youngster and bore down on Crompton's goal before passing to Grant, who had all the time in the world to control it, and he prodded it home as Chilton and Aston fruitlessly chased back.

The falling rain, which was slowly turning into snow, made the day even more miserable for the United support, and many had left the ground when Byrne pulled a goal back for United four minutes from time. A Rowley centre from the right was missed by Pearson and the ball went wide, but, for some unknown reason, the referee pointed to the penalty spot. Perhaps he was feeling sorry for the dejected red-shirted players. Byrne made no mistake and scored.

It certainly wasn't the best of afternoons for anyone to make their League debut, never mind a 16-year-old, and through no fault of his own Edwards failed to reappear in any of the remaining five games of that season.

In the following season, 1953–54, Edwards replaced Henry Cockburn against Huddersfield away on 31 October and never looked back, maturing into a player with immense natural ability. Such was his versatility that he was called upon to fill a number of roles and never once seemed out of place.

Edwards went on to establish himself not only with Manchester United but also in the England side, adding to his nine schoolboy caps with appearances in the England Youth and England B squads. There were also six appearances with the Under-23 team along with 18 for the full England side, his debut coming against Scotland in April 1955 when only 18 years and 183 days old.

With United Edwards gained two First Division Championship medals and an FA Cup runners'-up medal to accompany his three FA Youth Cup medals, making 175 appearances and scoring 21 goals.

Over the years, following his tragic death at Munich, there have been thousands of words written and spoken about Duncan Edwards, all of which sum him up as being the best player of his generation, destined to become one of the world greats, or possibly even the greatest.

Today many make the pilgrimage to the Black Country and to Dudley to visit his grave in the local cemetery andd to see the stained-glass windows in St Francis' Church, the exhibition of his caps and medals in the Dudley Museum and his statue in the town's high street.

The legend that is Duncan Edwards will never be forgotten.

Manchester United: Crompton, Aston, Byrne, Gibson, Chilton, Edwards, Berry, Rowley, Taylor, Pearson, Pegg.
Scorer: Byrne (penalty).
Cardiff City: Howells, Sherwood, Mansell, Hollyman, Montgomery, Blair, Tiddy, Williams, Grant, Chisholm, Northcott.
Scorers: Grant 2, Chisholm, Tiddy.
Attendance: 37,163.

No. 6

LIVERPOOL V UNITED

22 August 1953

When the new season fixture lists come out every summer they are eagerly scanned for the names of a select few opponents, clubs that can fall into the category of 'rivals', with those extra-special encounters sending a tingle down the spine as they draw close and enthralling encounters of yesteryear are remembered. The match days themselves add a skip to the step, with defeat something that is not even considered.

The local derby against Manchester City is one such encounter, but when our neighbours were busy contesting fixtures in a different League, another club emerged as the one every United supporter wanted to beat above all others, mainly due to their somewhat continued success throughout the 70s and 80s. That club was Liverpool.

Today it would certainly cause an interesting debate as to which one takes on the most importance, with City once again attempting to muscle in on the teams considered to be the biggest in the country.

In the early 1950s Liverpool did not cause United much in the way of problems. Indeed, between the resumption of League football in season 1946–47 following World War Two and the Anfield club's relegation at the end of season 1953–54, United only lost two of the 16 fixtures between the two sides, with Liverpool also failing to score in eight of those. Their trophy cabinet was also used for more advantageous things.

Relationships between the two clubs in the 1950s were a far cry from what they are today and certainly what they have been over the past couple of decades, even though United had tempted Matt Busby away from Anfield towards the end of World War Two, when Liverpool had offered their former player and captain the job of assistant manager.

Busby was a highly thought-of individual at Anfield, having made 122 appearances and scored three goals over four seasons, and formed what many consider as Liverpool's best-ever half-back line of Busby, McDougall and Bradshaw. It was also more than a possibility that he would have replaced George Kay as manager and could have been plotting United's downfall and bringing silverware to the Anfield trophy cabinet long before the days of Bill Shankly.

Had the opening two fixtures of season 1953–54 been in modern times, there would have been questions asked as to who was responsible and why, because United opened against Chelsea at Old Trafford and then travelled to Anfield to face Liverpool. To start the season with two of United's biggest rivals in consecutive games in a three-day period would certainly raise eyebrows now. To be honest, they were certainly not as bad as those for the previous season, when United had Chelsea at

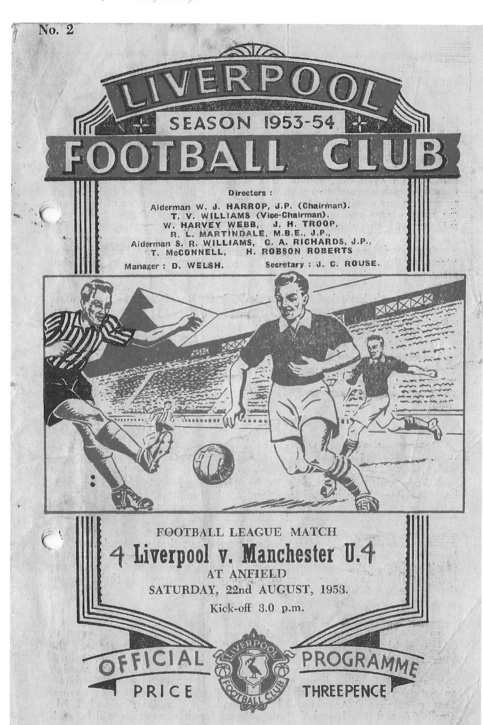

home, Arsenal away, City away and then Arsenal at home in the opening four fixtures. Back in the 50s, however, the prospect of those two such fixtures opening the campaign would have caused little anxiety within the confines of Old Trafford, as both Chelsea and Liverpool had finished in the lower half of the table in the previous season, with United in eighth.

Chelsea travelled north on the opening day, or rather the opening night, as the season got under way on Wednesday 19 August. They surprised United with a sterling performance and held them to a 1–1 draw.

Three days later it was off down the East Lancs Road to Anfield, which certainly wasn't the cauldron of hate that it is today, with the 46,725 who clicked through the turnstiles unaware of to the drama that lay in wait.

Matt Busby was forced into making one change from the opening fixture against Chelsea, bringing in 18-year-old former Manchester Schoolboy star Eddie Lewis in place of the injured captain, Stan Pearson. There was also a change of colours, with United taking to the field in blue shirts.

The game didn't get off to the best of starts for United as Henry Cockburn was injured in the opening 10 seconds. Intercepting the ball between Payne and Baron, he turned and attempted to clear the ball up-field but was tackled rather forcibly by Liverpool left-back Spicer, although the referee saw nothing wrong with the challenge and allowed play to continue. Spicer sent the ball into the United area, where Crompton did well to clear under pressure. Fortunately for United, Cockburn was able to resume after treatment from Tom Curry.

Forcing three successive corners, United had the Liverpool defence under pressure, and in the ninth minute they finally managed to break the deadlock, but only after a Liddell cross was headed narrowly past the post by Bimpson. The persistence of Eddie Lewis, chasing back to rob a Liverpool player of possession, began a free-flowing cross-field move as he slipped the ball wide to Tommy Taylor. The burly centre-forward in turn found Rowley, who kept up the momentum with a pass out to Pegg on the left. As Rowley moved forward Pegg judged his low cross perfectly, with the ball eluding the home defence, allowing Rowley to smash it home from an acute angle.

Taylor almost made it two with a shot that flew narrowly over, but Liverpool quickly counter-attacked and a free-kick into the United penalty area saw Bimpson out-jump Chilton, but his header was somehow pushed past by Crompton for a corner, which came to nothing.

Play moved quickly from end to end, but it was United who always looked the more dangerous, and the Liverpool support breathed a huge sigh of relief when Berry slipped as he was about to shoot when ideally positioned in front of goal.

Those sighs were soon to turn to cheers as Liverpool snatched an equaliser in the 20th minute, following a mistake by Jack Crompton. Full-back John Aston had been keeping a watchful eye on the tricky Billy Liddell, but he was unable to prevent the winger sending over a long, curling centre towards the far post. Crompton jumped and actually got his hands to the ball, but he somehow allowed it to drop from his grasp and into the back of the net.

A second United defensive error, this time by Allenby Chilton, almost gave Liverpool a second goal. The big centre-half completely missed his kick and allowed the ball to run to Blimpson. From around 10 yards out the Liverpool centre-forward unleashed a tremendous drive as Crompton moved forward to narrow the angle, and the ball flew narrowly over the crossbar.

For a while it was all Liverpool as a barrage of shots flashed towards the United goal, but somehow they were all blocked or went narrowly past. United did try to combat the threats with rather sporadic attacks of their own, but, rather surprisingly, it was not until a minute before the interval that the home side actually increased their lead, and once again it was something of a gift.

There seemed to be little danger to the United goal as both Chilton and Aston got to the ball before Bimpson, but the pass back forced Crompton into scrambling for the ball, and although the 'keeper got his hands to it he once again managed to let it slip from his grasp. Liddell was quickly on the ball and flicked it forward to Jones, who had the easiest of tasks scoring Liverpool's second.

Having started the game promisingly, United now found themselves behind, but within four minutes of the restart they were back on level-pegging thanks to a penalty decision by the referee. In those early second-half exchanges Taylor hesitated in front of goal when he should have done better, while Crompton redeemed himself a little with an excellent stop from Liddell. It was a push in the back of the United centre-forward as he was being chased by Lambert and Hughes that brought the spot-kick.

With Tommy Taylor having missed a penalty against Chelsea, the United support in the Anfield crowd were wondering who would take it, when up stepped left-back Roger Byrne to send his right-footed shot high into the Liverpool net, wide of the outstretched hands of Ashcroft.

Unfortunately the equaliser didn't herald United's revitalisation as Liverpool's good luck continued, and they scored two goals in as many minutes. The first came in the 55th minute, when danger-man Liddell, some 35 yards out, lobbed the ball into the United goalmouth. Crompton jumped and pushed the ball to one side, but the referee had judged it to have crossed the line for a corner. Despite the United 'keeper's protests the decision stood, and from the corner Blimpson headed home.

Liverpool quickly regained possession from the restart, and the ball was again forced out to Liddell. This time his cross caught Byrne unsighted, and it bounced off the full-back's body and into the net.

Down but certainly not out, United had plenty to do in order to get back into the game, and on the hour mark they pulled it back to 4–3. Berry's centre was controlled perfectly by Eddie Lewis, who proceeded to shoot past Ashcroft.

It was now game on as United fought tooth and nail for the equaliser and perhaps the opportunity to grasp a winner. Cockburn and Chilton were kept busy as they attempted to repel the Liverpool attacks, while the defenders were also quick to join in with any United counter-attacks that materialised.

With six minutes remaining United finally got the break they deserved. The ball was lobbed into the Liverpool goalmouth, coming down just under the crossbar, and as Ashcroft reached up to grab it he was bundled into the net, along with the ball, by Tommy Taylor. The Liverpool players vigorously protested to the referee, but he allowed the goal to stand. In hindsight the Liverpool 'keeper should have played safe and punched the ball over the bar.

Allenby Chilton, the United centre-half, was the man who almost had the last say in how the game would end, as with only two minutes remaining he was at hand to head Lambert's cross over the bar for a corner, while at the opposite end his header from a United corner went straight into the arms of Ashcroft, who was relived that on this occasion there was no one following through.

Roger Byrne.

It was with some disappointment that the final whistle blew, as the 90 minutes had provided the best game seen at Anfield for a long time. Along with the eight goals, there were countless near misses. In the end, however, neither side deserved to lose.

Despite the sterling play against Liverpool, the overall performance in the opening half of season 1953–54 was rather poor, and it was not until the ninth game of the campaign that United recorded their first victory, a 4–1 win over Middlesbrough at Ayresome Park. This, however, wasn't the result that would kick-start the season as the inconsistency continued, and it was November before they actually won two games in a row, beating Cardiff City 6–1 and Blackpool 4–1. Ten goals came in two games when they had only scored 21 in the previous 17!

True to form, United failed to win any of their next three matches, but then came a repeat performance of another 10 goals in two games – an emphatic 5–1 thumping of Liverpool at Old Trafford, followed by 5–2 against Sheffield Wednesday on Christmas Day six days later, again at home.

At this time Liverpool were anchored at the foot of the First Division, and their defeat against United wasn't helped by the fact that they fielded two debutants in goalkeeper Underwood and centre-half Twentyman, two crucial defensive areas. Their cause was further hampered when their left-back, Spicer, broke his leg tackling Tommy Taylor as the United centre-forward was about to score United's opening goal in the 14th minute.

Reduced to 10 men, Liverpool could put up little resistance, and by half-time United were leading 4–0 through Taylor (2), Blanchflower and Viollet. They did manage to pull one back in the 58th minute, but it was to be a mere consolation as Blanchflower grabbed a second 11 minutes from the end in a rather one-sided game.

Despite United's inconsistent performances over most of the season, they somehow managed to climb to fourth in the League, finishing nine points behind champions Wolves. Liverpool, however, failed rather miserably, propping up the table, having won only nine of their 42 games. Relegation to the Second Division beckoned for them.

Manchester United: Crompton, Aston, Byrne, Gibson, Chilton, Cockburn, Berry, Rowley, Taylor, Pearson, Pegg.
Scorers: Rowley, Byrne (penalty), Lewis, Taylor.
Liverpool: Ashcroft, Lambert, Spicer, Taylor, Hughes, Paisley, Payne, Baron, Blimpson, Jones, Liddell.
Scorers: Liddell, Jones, Blimpson, Byrne (own-goal).
Attendance: 46,725.

No. 7

HUDDERSFIELD TOWN V UNITED

31 October 1953

Matt Busby, having managed to turn the nucleus of his 1948 Cup-winning side into First Division champions in 1952, now faced possibly an even more demanding task. Those heroes of both campaigns – Jack Crompton, John Aston, Allenby Chilton, Henry Cockburn, Stan Pearson and Jack Rowley – still clung onto their first-team places as season 1953–54 kicked off. However, they were now into the twilight stages of their careers, although Chilton still managed to play in all 42 League games and Jack Rowley in 36, but the eventual need for replacements was always a recurring thought in the United manager's mind. How would he rebuild his aging side?

Tommy Taylor had already been prised away from Barnsley for a fee of £29,999, a considerable sum at that particular time, while Johnny Berry, always a thorn in the side of Busby's team whenever he faced them as a Birmingham City player, had been signed in September 1951 for a mere £15,000. But the Manchester United of the 1950s as not an exceptionally wealthy club, and although money was available for transfers, Busby had a completely different vision as to the future of his club.

The 1953–54 season had begun with five draws and three defeats in the opening eight games, and it wasn't until 16 September that the first victory was recorded, 4–1 away at Middlesbrough. This, however, did not exactly bring a change in fortune as the following five fixtures produced two wins, two defeats and a draw.

A casual glance at the First Division table, with 15 games played, saw United some 12 points behind early leaders West Bromwich Albion but only six points ahead of bottom club Sunderland. It was still early days, but there had been enough evidence to nudge Busby into taking some form of action sooner rather than later.

'How can football sink so low as in this game at Old Trafford?' questioned one correspondent following United's 1–0 victory over Aston Villa on 24 October. Whether or not Busby read that particular report is not known, but with a friendly arranged at Kilmarnock four days later he replaced the evergreen Stan Pearson and Jack Rowley with the promising talents of Jackie Blanchflower and Dennis Viollet.

Blanchflower, a 19-year-old Irishman who had been turning out for the Central League side at centre-forward, had made his debut at Anfield in November 1951 alongside another youngster making his first appearance in the United senior side, Roger Byrne. Viollet, on the other hand, was a local-born talent and a former England Schoolboy internationalist who had

HUDDERSFIELD TOWN

Association Football Club
Ltd.

OFFICIAL
PROGRAMME

3D

LEEDS ROAD, HUDDERSFIELD

recently been demobbed from the army and who had made his initial appearance in the first team at Newcastle as recently as April 1953.

Under the newly installed floodlights at Kilmarnock, the visitors thrilled the crowd of 16,000 with an entertaining display, playing fluent, attacking football while showing a vastly superior array of skills and close ball control, and although the game was classed as a friendly it was vigorously contested throughout.

Such was the competitiveness of the encounter that Cockburn, scorer of the first United goal in the 3–0 Rugby Park victory, received an injury that saw a third relatively untried youngster by the name of Duncan Edwards, a mere 17-year-old, thrown into the fray. Despite his tender years he was a player destined for greatness, with his name having already been pencilled in as a future England international even before he had made his United first-team debut in April 1953 against Cardiff City.

The victory at Kilmarnock and the manner in which it had been achieved gave Busby much to think about on the journey back to Manchester, and it came as little surprise that all three players brought into the side on the Ayrshire coast kept their places the following Saturday as United headed over the Pennines to Leeds Road, Huddersfield, on First Division business. There were a few doubters, however, who felt that Busby was perhaps taking something of a gamble for this particular fixture because the home side were third in the League, three points behind the leaders.

Despite the slight immaturity and inexperience of Busby's selected 11, they held their own against their more battle-hardened opponents, and although the game ended without any goals it saw the birth of what was to become a legendary name in world football. It was the rather innocuous heading of 'Busby's Bouncing "Babes" Keep All Town Awake' above the *Manchester Evening Chronicle* report by Alf Clarke, the United correspondent, and a man who had reported on the highs and the lows of the Old Trafford side for a considerable number of years, which caught the eye and was to become fabled from that day to this.

The heading has always been credited to the man from the *Chronicle*, but, in a time when a football correspondent's life was not an easy one, it is debatable that while Clarke was shouting his report down the phone line to some copywriter that he also had the time to conjure up his match-report headings. Could it have been some unknown, sitting in a Manchester office, who coined the memorable name? Nevertheless, the 'Busby Babes' were born, and although Busby himself is said to have taken something of a dislike to it, it was ideal.

As the game got under way, it was United who took the initiative and came close to taking an early lead when Berry sent a tantalising cross into the Huddersfield penalty area, but goalkeeper Mills just managed to pluck the ball off the head of Tommy Taylor. Continuing to press, further crosses from Byrne and Rowley ensured that the home defence were kept fully occupied.

At the opposite end, Glazzard, Huddersfield's major goal threat, was closely marked by Chilton, although he did manage to get the better of the United man on one occasion only to find the veteran defender's reactions were still 100%, and an outstretched leg managed to divert the ball to Whitefoot, who cleared up-field. Staniforth also had the United support holding

Jack Rowley.

its breath as he broke through unchallenged, but a sigh of relief could be heard around the ground as Crompton dealt comfortably with the Huddersfield full-back's shot.

As the game progressed, what of the trio of relative newcomers in the red shirts? A fine piece of play by Viollet in the 14th minute almost gave United the breakthrough that they sought. After gaining possession in midfield, he lobbed the ball through towards Taylor, and a slip by Huddersfield defender McEvoy gave the former Barnsley centre-forward the time and the space to bring the ball under control, but with the goal practically at his mercy he somehow managed to steer the ball over the bar.

Edwards and Blanchflower were combining well in midfield with the former heading clear, although the ball was soon back into the United area, with Chilton this time needed to perform the heroics to keep the scoreline blank. Blanchflower, on the other hand, just failed to connect with a Berry free-kick, the ball being scrambled away by Huddersfield left-back Howe. But it was the Dudley youngster who was catching the eye, with Alf Clarke writing in his report, 'Edwards was coming more into the game the longer it went on. His stamina for a 17-year-old is something terrific.'

Huddersfield's play confirmed their League position as they displayed a wide array of talent, swiftly moving from defence into attack, although at times they were quite content to send a long ball forward towards centre-forward Glazzard in the hope that he would get the better of Chilton or else force the United centre-half into making a mistake.

One poor clearance by Chilton almost proved disastrous as the ball was collected by Huddersfield's Scottish international inside-forward Jimmy Watson, who then passed it out to Metcalfe in plenty of space with time to bring it under control. Fortunately for United he placed his shot just inches wide of the far post. The Huddersfield outside-left also came close minutes later, dummying Foulkes before cutting inside, but on this occasion his shot was saved by the well-positioned Wood.

Although it could be considered something of an even game, the home side did seem to have that little bit extra in attack, but they simply could not convert those opportunities into goals. United were equally inconsistent in front of goal, and in the opening 45 minutes even Ray Wood tried his luck at goal on a couple of occasions, using the wind to his advantage, with two of his clearances travelling the length of the field. His aim was slightly out, however, as the ball bounced out of play nearer to the corner flag than the Huddersfield goal. At least he did not suffer any embarrassment from his efforts, unlike Byrne, who sent the ball out of the ground with one attempt as the first half drew to a close.

Byrne was also in the thick of the action as the second half got under way. He firstly came to the rescue with a well-timed tackle on Glazzard but then unnecessarily found himself caught in possession and had to scramble the ball out for a corner to avert any immediate danger. Minutes later he would be found heading clear a tantalising cross from Metcalfe.

Huddersfield were beginning to enjoy much of the play, putting the United goal under siege, but to their credit the visitors' defence stood firm and somehow managed to prevent the ball from finding its way past Wood, although he was beaten by a Davie header and could only watch as the ball flashed inches over the crossbar.

With the United defenders standing firm under the barrage of Huddersfield attacks, it was down to the red-shirted forwards to up their game in the attempt to relieve some of that pressure. Howe kicked the ball off Taylor's toes when a goal looked certain, while not long after this Viollet spurned the best opportunity of the game. Clean-through on goal, with only Mills in the Huddersfield goal to beat, he rushed his shot, kicking it straight at the 'keeper's body. Unable to hold the ball, it rebounded towards the on-running Taylor and again the crowd anticipated a goal, but somehow Staniforth managed to block it and Mills finally managed to scramble it clear.

Moving into the final stages, United looked as if they might well snatch a victory. Taylor found Edwards with a neat back pass, but although the Dudley youngster managed to get his shot on target it lacked the power to beat Mills.

While Rowley on the United left was rather subdued through lack of service, Berry on the right was a constant pain in Huddersfield's side and received warm applause from the appreciative crowd for two magnificent runs. Neither managed to conjure up the illusive goal though, and the game came to a close with the score sheet blank.

It is not often a goalless draw finds it way into a list of memorable matches, but this particular fixture is considered by everyone as the birth of the 'Babes' and plays more than a significant part in the history of Manchester United Football Club.

Manchester United: Wood, Foulkes, Byrne, Whitefoot, Chilton, Edwards, Berry, Blanchflower, Taylor, Viollet, Rowley.
Huddersfield Town: Mills, Staniforth, Howe, McGarry, McEvoy, Quested, Gunn, Watson, Glazzard, Davie, Metcalfe.
Attendance: 34,175.

No. 8
BURNLEY V UNITED
9 January 1954

Seasons 1953–54 and 1954–55 were somewhat transitional in the immediate post-war history of Manchester United. The old guard of the 1948 FA Cup-winning side were nearing the end of their days on the Old Trafford stage, while Busby had begun the injection of youth into the ranks in the form of Roger Byrne, Jackie Blanchflower, Dennis Viollet, Ray Wood, Bill Foulkes, David Pegg and the incomparable Duncan Edwards.

It was something of a slow process as results didn't always go United's way, but Busby stuck to his guns with his youngsters, determined that his vision and belief would pay off, and if defeats came their way then so be it – it was all part of the learning process. One week they lost 3–1 at Stamford Bridge and then seven days later took five off Liverpool at Old Trafford. A month later it was a heavy 5–1 defeat at home to Bolton Wanderers; the next week, they travelled the short distance to Preston North End's Deepdale and won 3–1. Consistency was nowhere to be seen, but at least it provided the supporters with plenty to talk about – cringe-worthy performances and, of course, entertainment, even if the latter was on a rather irregular basis.

The 3–1 defeat by Chelsea was the first reversal in seven games (three wins and four draws) and was followed by a further five unbeaten games (four wins and a draw), taking United into 1954 hoping that the new year was going to produce more of the same and perhaps even an extended run in the FA Cup.

Drawn against Burnley at Turf Moor in the third round, the Cup would bring a welcome relief to the rigours of the weekly First Division grind, but, having lost 2–1 at Old Trafford back in October, Matt Busby knew that the near neighbours could prove to be something of a handful.

F.A. CUP—3rd ROUND
**BURNLEY v.
MANCHESTER UTD.**
Saturday, 9th January, 1954
To be RETAINED. | Kick-off 2-15 p.m.

10653

Coming on the back of a 2–1 win at Newcastle, which saw Bill Foulkes score his first United goal with a freak 40-yard lob over the head of the unsuspecting Simpson, United were well-prepared, mentally at least, for the short journey to Turf Moor, even though they had only won once in the three previous Cup encounters there.

While the events of that January afternoon would not compare to those of 1908–09, when snow saw the quarter-final tie between the two clubs being abandoned with only 18 minutes remaining, with Burnley leading 1–0, only for United to win the rearranged fixture 3–2, this

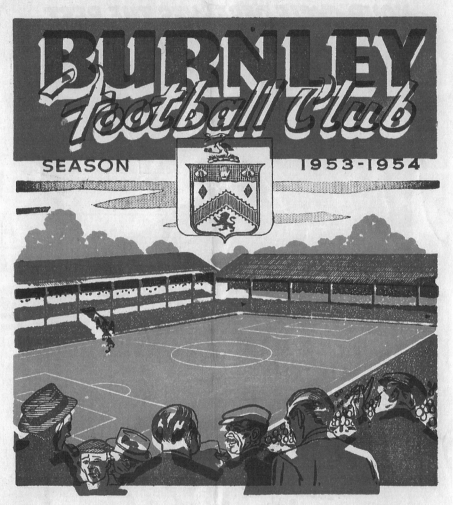

particular 90 minutes would become etched in the memories of the 54,000 who were in attendance for some time to come.

United were unchanged for the seventh consecutive game, and following an overnight thaw the pitch was rather heavy and well sanded, the latter causing the pre-kick-off toss-up to be done twice because the first attempt saw the coin land sideways in the soft surface of the centre circle.

For those who left it late in getting into the ground, whether due to congestion at the turnstiles, transport difficulties or simply in no hurry to dash from the warmth of the pub into the cold afternoon air, it was to prove a grave mistake.

It was United who mounted the first real attack of the afternoon, and as they advanced towards the home goal Whitefoot was brought crashing to the ground rather unceremoniously by McIlroy. The resulting free-kick, however, came to nothing, and Burnley were immediately on the counter-attack. McIlroy and Holden exchanged passes down the right before the former crossed into the United area, where Shannon, racing through between Chilton and Edwards, headed the ball wide of Wood's right hand and into the back of the net. A mere two minutes had gone and United were a goal behind. Three minutes later it was 2–0. Mather kicked the ball off the Burnley goalline, and it soared through the air towards Holden who, although in his own half of the pitch, raced through the stranded and static United defence to beat Wood with ease. The home crowd were ecstatic, while on the pitch the Burnley players must have thought that they had the game well in control and, even though there were still some 85 minutes to go, were now wondering who they might get in the fourth-round draw.

Things, however, suddenly took a much different outlook with a further two goals in as many minutes. From the restart, Berry, in the centre, passed the ball wide to Taylor, and along with Viollet they worked the ball down-field. The United centre then crossed into the middle, with Viollet turning the ball into the net. Then in the eighth minute Taylor, again in the thick of the action and still out wide on the right, went racing down the wing, chasing a ball that looked to be going out of play. Catching it just as it neared the byline, the centre-forward crossed into the Burnley area, where Aird, under pressure from Blanchflower, attempted to pass the ball back to his 'keeper but only succeeded in steering it into his own net.

Four goals in seven minutes and suddenly what looked to be a Burnley walkover now saw United as the most dangerous of the two sides, although it was only the foot of Ray Wood that prevented the home side from taking a 3–2 lead, blocking a goal-bound shot from McIlroy.

At the opposite end Rowley lobbed the ball into the centre, where Cummings and Thompson hesitated, leaving the ball for each other, but the United forwards failed to capitalise on the goalkeeper and centre-half's hesitation, and the 'keeper quickly gathered the ball to avert the immediate danger.

It was the home side who were to take the lead again in the 18th minute with something of a fluke goal. Shannon seemed to lose his footing as he moved down the right but managed to keep control of the ball almost at the corner flag. His attempted cross hit Foulkes on the head and flew high into the air. Wood, in the United goal, had been covering his near post and was caught out of position, and the ball dropped under the crossbar, through his hands and into the net. It was a disappointing goal to lose but that is football, and with the conditions underfoot pushing the players to the limit it was becoming everything a Cup tie should be.

A miraculous save from Thompson in the 25th minute coupled with another shortly afterwards prevented United from once again drawing level. Firstly the Burnley custodian's outstretched hand prevented Taylor's header from a Whitefoot cross from going in, and then he had to come racing out of his goal and give away a free-kick in a dangerous position by handling the ball outside the penalty area in an effort to prevent Berry from scoring.

The Burnley goal was by now coming under severe pressure but somehow managed to withstand whatever United threw their way as Whitefoot and Edwards provided excellent support for their forwards. Blanchflower was then forced onto the wing due to an injury received in yet another attack, while a minute before half-time Rowley found himself in front of goal only 10 yards out, but, with the crowd shouting 'Shoot', he held onto it for too long, allowing Mather to run in and kick the ball off his toes.

United could and perhaps should have gone in at the interval on level terms, but they had to wait until seven minutes after the restart before they could claim their third. Berry and Whitefoot moved the ball down the right and it was soon centred towards Blanchflower. His shot rebounded off a Burnley defender but only to the feet of Taylor, who scooped it up with his foot before hitting it towards goal in the same movement. The ball flew past a helpless Thompson.

With almost an hour played, Pilkington, well positioned inside the United penalty area, should have given the home side the lead, but after managing to work his way past Whitefoot he put his shot wide of the goal. Two further opportunities came the Burnley outside-left's way, but his first effort was saved by Wood while the second went high over the bar.

The playing conditions were slowly deteriorating, making close control difficult, but it certainly did not prevent both sides from continuing in their search for goals. Blanchflower saw a long-range effort well saved by Thompson, then a pass from Byrne to Taylor saw the United centre-forward out-manoeuvre Cummings 10 yards inside the Burnley half. Racing towards the Burnley goal, Byrne had his legs unceremoniously kicked from underneath him. There was to be no justice, however, as Berry's free-kick was easily cleared.

Shannon shot wide for Burnley, but in the 67th minute the home side gained the advantage. Holden moved wide on the left, where he beat Foulkes before crossing into the United area. McIlroy managed to get to the ball quicker than anyone else and dribbled round three United defenders in the space of about four yards before driving the ball past Wood, who struggled even to move towards the ball in the muddy goalmouth.

Burnley had concentrated most of their second-half attacks down the United left, and countless crosses from this side of the pitch bombarded the visitors' goal, but it was from a free-kick that their fifth goal came. Chilton fouled Holden six yards outside the United area, and as one Burnley player ran over the ball McIlroy tapped it to the side of the United defensive wall, where Gray was onto the ball and tapped it past Wood as he advanced from his line.

Two goals behind and with 20 minutes of play remaining, United still had the opportunity to rescue something from the game. But as the minutes ticked slowly away, it became obvious that the visitors were tiring, and even forcing a replay was beyond them. Rowley did come close to pulling one goal back in the final minute when he sent a powerful drive goalwards, but Thompson was more than equal to it, plucking the ball out of the air with ease.

As the final whistle sounded the crowd rose in their acclaim of both sides for their part in making this Cup tie such a memorable encounter. The scene was perhaps best described by the excellent Don Davies, 'Old International' of the *Manchester Guardian*. He wrote, 'When the end came, with the Burnley gladiators tired but happily in command, youths poured from the ground in a mad race to be the first to take the news to the stay-at-homes waiting anxiously at their street doors. The streets became alive with homely folk wearing smiles as broad as their broad bosoms. Elderly men stood silent in pairs and with hands clasped, with that intent look in their eyes as of veterans who have lived through many battles, but never a battle like this one. Even the Manchester supporters wore their drooping favours with a proud air, for if ever a team went down with its colours flying, that team was Manchester United. Those youngsters gave all they had – courage in diversity, steadiness under strain, the gallantry to draw level after three successive shocks, and the ability to flog their weary limbs into one supreme effort when all seemed lost. But there was one thing that might have saved them – the wisdom that comes only with experience.'

The following day's newspapers were just as praiseworthy in their headlines: 'So Thrilling It Was Almost Exhausting', 'Conquered by Burnley Stamina', '22 Won Glory In Cup Battle to Remember' were just three such headings from the national press, although the *Guardian* was a bit more forthright with their heading, 'Moments of Madness at Burnley.'

In the *Daily Herald*, George Follows described the 90 minutes as 'the finest Cup game I ever saw,' but he was also quick to put his finger on the reason why Manchester United were not in the fourth round. 'People who weren't there will be asking: Did Matt Busby blunder in throwing five youngsters into the fiery furnace of their first Cup game at Burnley?

'No, sir, he didn't.

'Indeed, Manchester United lost not because they were too young, but because they were too old.

'Nobody wants to throw brickbats after this triumph of human skill and endeavour over clinging mud and the soccer-destroying tension of the Cup. But this must be said of the United: The Busby Boys were let down by the men.' He finished his summary with the following: 'But for me the final memory will be of the boy Edwards striding through the mud in hopeless battle, the bravest man on the field.' Matt Busby kept faith with his youngsters, and, although results didn't always go his way, the defeat at Burnley being followed by a 1–1 draw at home to City and the 5–1 defeat by Bolton Wanderers, also at home, he knew what he was doing and where his team were going, with the 5–3 Cup defeat at Burnley becoming nothing more than a mention in the history books.

Manchester United: Wood, Foulkes, Byrne, Whitefoot, Chilton, Edwards, Berry, Blanchflower, Taylor, Viollet, Rowley.
Scorers: Viollet, Aird (own-goal), Taylor.
Burnley: Thompson, Aird, Mather, Adamson, Cummings, Atwell, Gray, McIlroy, Holden, Shannon, Pilkington.
Scorers: Shannon 2, Holden, McIlroy, Gray.
Attendance: 54,218.

No. 9

CHELSEA V UNITED

16 October 1954

The record books show that United only managed to finish fifth in the First Division in season 1954–55, and it is more than a possibility that three straight defeats in February 1955 – 5–0 at home against Manchester City, 4–2, again at home, against Wolverhampton Wanderers, and 3–0 at Cardiff City's Ninian Park – were much to blame. Those defeats saw them drop from third, when they were a mere two points behind leaders Sunderland, to sixth, only to drop lower with a further two reversals against Sunderland, 4–3 at Roker Park, and Leicester City, 1–0 at Filbert Street, in early April, confirming their place among the also-rans for yet another year.

It was, however, only a drop of one place on the previous season, and despite the rather ordinary showing there were a few creditable performances from individuals and the team as a whole, while it was also the season that really made people sit up and begin to recognise that Matt Busby was on the verge of having a team to be reckoned with, a team built on youth, with strong foundations for the future.

Season 1954–55 got under way in the worst possible manner, a 3–1 defeat at home to Portsmouth. 'Rain and Goal Flood Hits United,' proclaimed the headline on the front page of the *Manchester Evening Chronicle's Football Pink* for Saturday 21 August. A tropical rainstorm over Old Trafford saw many vacate the wide, open terracing for whatever cover they could find, while others simply left for home. Women and children were caught up in the stampede, with the police and ambulance men standing helpless.

Such were the conditions that the referee had to inspect the pitch prior to the second half commencing, but unfortunately for United he decided to let play resume, allowing the visitors to improve on their 1–0 lead. However, the defeat seemed to kick-start Matt Busby's team into action and they won six of their next eight fixtures; drawing the other two.

The first Manchester derby of the season on 25 September saw City triumph 3–2 at Maine Road, with a visit to Molineux the following Saturday bringing a 4–2 defeat. Cardiff City travelled to Old Trafford seven days later on 9 October, feeling confident that they could add to United's woes, but they returned to South Wales empty-handed on the end of a 5–2 defeat, Tommy Taylor rediscovering his scoring form with four. United hadn't managed to score five in a League game since December 1953 when they did so on consecutive Saturdays against Liverpool (5–1) and Sheffield Wednesday (5–2), both games played at Old Trafford.

Following the rout of Cardiff City, United travelled to Stamford Bridge to face Chelsea, with the Pensioners having held League leaders West Bromwich Albion to a 3–3 draw at the

Chelsea
Football Club

Stamford Bridge Grounds, London SW6

FOOTBALL LEAGUE—DIVISION I

CHELSEA
v
MANCHESTER UNITED

Saturday, 16th October, 1954   Kick-off 3 p.m.

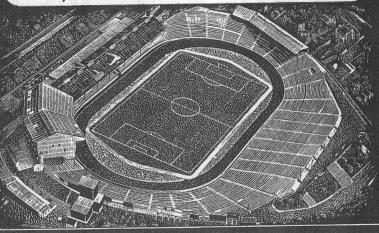

Official Programme **6d** The right of admission to grounds is reserved.

Tommy Taylor.

same time as United were hammering five past the Welshmen.

Not having won on the road for three games wasn't exactly promising form, and trawling through the archives, you find on the back of a report for United's thrashing of Cardiff the football pools forecasts for Saturday 16 October, which shows that that particular newspaper thought that United would manage a draw. With Chelsea not having won in their last four, this was perhaps not a bad assumption.

Fortunately for both sides, neither had any Welsh or Scottish players in their first-choice 11 because the two countries were taking part in their first home international match of the season at Ninian Park, and in those distant days clubs simply had to grin and bear it if they had players called up for international duty. On that particular day Arsenal had four of their players in the Welsh side but still had to face Portsmouth at Highbury. Needless to say, they lost, although only 1–0.

United had no such worries, and Matt Busby fielded the same team that had beaten Cardiff, with centre-half Allenby Chilton playing his 150th consecutive League game for the club, a feat that had never before been achieved. Chelsea, on the other hand, included two amateur internationalists on the left wing in O'Connell and Lewis, the former making his League debut.

The Chelsea goal was under threat almost from the kick-off, with a clearance from Blanchflower sending Taylor scurrying forward. Greenwood rushed in to tackle as the United centre shot for goal and, with everyone expecting the referee to award a corner, he gave a goal-kick. Moments later it was Viollet moving through on goal, but a challenge from Willemse was enough to prevent the United player from getting too much power and direction behind his shot and it went narrowly past the post.

A foul on Taylor saw Rowley's free-kick fly across the Chelsea penalty area, and although Taylor managed to get his head to the ball it went just wide of the post.

Play moved endlessly from one goalmouth to the other, but without either 'keeper being really troubled.

Chilton misjudged the flight of the ball, presenting McNichol with a chance, but Gibson got in a tackle and the United centre-half, having regained position, cleared the ball to safety. A long centre from Parsons then saw Wood race from his goal and collect the ball, but, to the surprise of the crowd and his teammates, he dropped it. Fortunately he recovered in time to pounce before anyone else got to it.

The first goal materialised in the 15th minute. A corner from Johnny Berry was cleared by Willemse but was quickly redispatched towards the Chelsea goal by Foulkes. The ball then hit Harris and bounced towards Taylor. Unable to bring the ball under control, it rolled into the path of Viollet, who got his toe to it and prodded it home.

Within five minutes, however, Chelsea were level. A centre shot from Parsons saw Wood having to dive at the feet of Bentley. Then Foulkes, who had ample time to clear a bouncing ball, missed it completely. The ball rolled to Bentley who, when Foulkes tried to redeem his mistake by tackling the Chelsea centre-forward, slipped it sideways to O'Connell who, with an open goal in front of him, made no mistake.

United's defensive play was rather haphazard, and Bentley continued to create problems. Having moved out to the left, he cut in along the byline and, when around six yards from Wood, crossed the ball into the crowded United goalmouth. It appeared to go underneath the United 'keeper's arms as he dived and ran to Lewis, who deflected it into the net to put Chelsea in front in the 32nd minute.

Six minutes later and it was 2–2. Having forced a corner on the right, Berry's kick went straight towards Tommy Taylor, who out-jumped everyone to send a powerful header past Robertson.

Having regained something of their momentum, United maintained the pressure on the Chelsea goal. A long clearance from Chilton saw Berry racing down the wing, closely pursued by Willemse, but it was the United man who reached the ball first and cut along the byline before slipping it back to Viollet, who could not fail to make it 3–2 in United's favour.

The five goals in an action-packed opening-45 minutes certainly gave the crowd value for money, but had they known what lay in store in the second half then they would have been expecting the gatemen back in place at full time, taking a collection for what they had just witnessed.

Johnny Berry.

Robertson had to race from his goal to thwart Viollet as the second half got under way, but he was forced to pick the ball out of his net within three minutes of the restart.

Johnny Berry was having one of his best games for United since moving from Birmingham City and, exchanging passes with Tommy Taylor, the United centre-forward sent the diminutive winger scurrying down the touchline. He went past Willemse before heading for goal and causing panic in the Chelsea defence. Looking up, he spotted Taylor and cut the ball back into his path, and seconds later it was in the Chelsea net.

Such was United's play that even the home support were warm in their acknowledgement, despite the scoreline. But their applause might have been a little less warm had United increased their lead to 5–2 when Rowley was put through by Viollet and could have found the lingering Taylor instead of kicking the ball into the arms of goalkeeper Robertson.

That fifth goal, however, was not long in coming. Almost on the hour mark, Berry, once again in the thick of the action, moved inside before passing to Viollet, who then ran at the Chelsea defence before hitting the ball firmly along the ground and past Robertson.

If any Chelsea supporters had thought enough was enough and decided to make their way home, heading for the exits and the first tube from Fulham Broadway (there was a bus strike on that day), then they had made a big mistake, as Armstrong reduced the difference in the 63rd minute when poor marking by the United defence allowed him to jump unmarked and head past Wood.

The fans might have contemplated the move a minute later, though, when Blanchflower scored United's sixth, deflecting home Berry's 12-yard shot with his head, but they would still have been missing out.

Straight from the restart Chelsea moved forward, and as the ball swung over from the right to the edge of the United penalty area O'Connell latched onto it and sent it past the unsighted Wood for Chelsea's fourth.

As if they sensed that there was still a possibility of grasping something from a game that at one stage looked like it was all over, Chelsea began pushing forward at every opportunity, with the crowd eagerly behind them.

With 10 minutes remaining Bentley centred the ball into the United area and Parsons headed against the post. Quickest to react was O'Connell, and the debutant notched his hat-trick, driving the ball past Wood.

As full time drew near, with Chelsea still pounding forward, they came close to claiming a

Jackie Blanchflower.

dramatic equaliser when Bentley, again in a wide position, lobbed the ball forward from a free-kick, but Wood managed to push it over the bar. As the corner-kick came over, Foulkes attempted to pass the ball back to Wood but failed to put enough power in it, and it took the quick reactions of United's 'keeper to beat O'Connell to the ball.

Considering the Chelsea of today have money to burn, so to speak, football in the 50s was so much different, which is clearly defined with their debutant scorer, Seamus O'Connell, a Carlisle cattle salesman, saying after the match that he had no intention of turning professional and intended to return to Bishop Auckland in December so that he could play in the FA Amateur Cup.

Had there been another five or 10 minutes to play, then who knows what the scoreline would have shown, but a quick look at his watch showed that the 90 minutes were indeed up and the referee's whistle signalled the end of one of the most exciting games ever to take place at Stamford Bridge. Another goal for the home side would also have seen the Football League record equalled, as Leicester City and Arsenal drew 6–6 on 21 April 1930.

As something of a consolation for losing such a closely fought encounter, Chelsea went on to win the First Division Championship for the first time, beating relegation-doomed Sheffield Wednesday on the penultimate day of the season. Ironically, the Londoners' first game as the newly crowned champions saw them travel to Old Trafford on the final day of the season, where United took great delight in beating them 2–1, with goals from Scanlon and Taylor.

Scanning through the archives, one article from the *News Chronicle* catches the eye and makes you wonder if pre-match habits played any part in United's Stamford Bridge victory. Frank Taylor wrote, 'The Busby Babes restaking their claim for soccer honours this season on – steaks. For years clubs have been taking their players for a meal of dry toast and anaemic-looking boiled fish before games. That's no diet for warriors…and now the Manchester United lads have a steak before a game, if they fancy it.

'Says Duncan Edwards, United's young man-mountain of a right-half, "With my appetite I feel just grand. I feel as though I have something to play on."'

Unfortunately the steaks did not play their part in any of the game's trophies ending up in the Old Trafford boardroom, but the future was certainly bright, with Busby's youngsters on the verge of greatness, the likes Whelan, Scanlon, Bent, Kennedy, Goodwin and Greaves all making their debuts during 1954–55, with many other in the pipeline.

Would they play in any games as eventful as this one?

Chelsea: Robertson, Harris, Willemse, Armstrong, Greenwood, Saunders, Parsons, McNichol, Bentley, S. O'Connell, J. Lewis.
Scorers: O'Connell 3, Lewis, Armstrong.
Manchester United: Wood, Foulkes, Byrne, Gibson, Chilton, Edwards, Berry, Blanchflower, Taylor, Viollet, Rowley.
Scorers: Viollet 3, Taylor 2, Blanchflower.
Attendance: 55,966.

No. 10
BRISTOL ROVERS V UNITED
7 January 1956

Since their FA Cup Final victory over Blackpool in 1948, United had struggled in the competition. They had reached the semi-finals in 1949, losing 1–0 in a replay to Wolves at Everton's Goodison Park, but other than that had found the competition far from their liking, particularly when they came face to face with clubs from a lesser division of the Football League.

It wasn't as if they could always blame their form of the time either, as often results had been favourable in the weeks before the Cup tie. There was just something about the competition that failed to bring out the best in Matt Busby's team. Thus, when the draw was made for the third round of the 1955–56 competition and the name 'Manchester United' came out after that of 'Bristol Rovers', there wasn't exactly much in the way of enthusiasm in the Old Trafford camp.

In the final four weeks of the year United had won six and lost two of their eight fixtures, with Dennis Viollet in prolific form, having scored eight of their 15 goals. A 2–1 victory over neighbours City on the last day of 1955 was ideal preparation for the forthcoming Cup tie.

Played in front of 60,956, Old Trafford's biggest gate since the war, United found themselves a goal behind at the interval, Dyson, looking more than suspiciously offside, having put the light-blue shirts ahead in the 28th minute. Twelve minutes into the second half United were level, Tommy Taylor latching onto a long clearance from Ray Wood that bounced over the head of Ewing, allowing the former Barnsley man to coolly lift the ball over the head of the advancing Trautmann.

This goal gave United the lift they needed and they proceeded to throw everything at the City defence. With 15 minutes remaining, a shot from Berry was deflected for a corner, rather needlessly by Little, when Trautmann was right behind him. David Pegg took the kick, hitting it low towards the City goal, where an unmarked Denis Viollet made little mistake, glancing it home.

Seven days later it was off to Bristol to face a Rovers team who were sitting joint top of the Second Division, a point behind their neighbours City, and who had prepared for the Cup tie by beating Sheffield Wednesday 4–2 on 31 December, although their recent form was anything but impressive, having won only three of the previous nine League games. But United's visit, their first to Eastville Stadium for a competitive fixture in 21 years, which United won 3–1, certainly brought the best out of them.

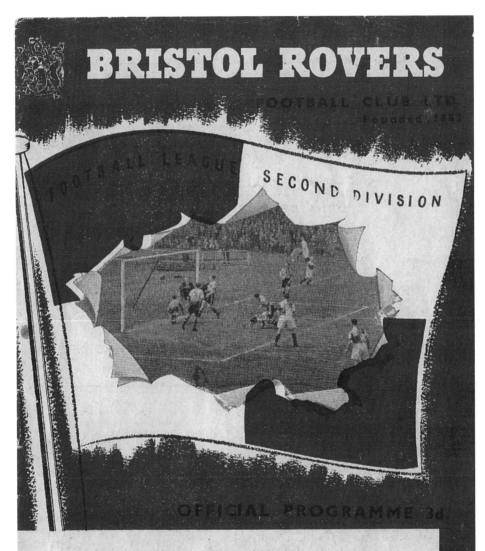

BRISTOL ROVERS

FOOTBALL CLUB LTD.
Founded 1883

FOOTBALL LEAGUE SECOND DIVISION

OFFICIAL PROGRAMME 3d.

PRESIDENT : HIS GRACE THE DUKE OF BEAUFORT K.G. P.C. G.C.V.O

DIRECTORS
H. J. HAMPDEN ALPASS (Chairman); J. P. HARE; P. W. HORT; DR. M. A. NICHOLSON;
E. A. SCUDAMORE; D. SIMPSON; CON. A. L. STEVENS.

MANAGER : B. J. TANN   **SECRETARY :** JOHN GUMMOW.

MEDICAL OFFICERS :
Dr. M. A. Nicholson M.B., Ch.B.   Dr. W. T. Cussen, M.B., Ch.B., B.A.O.,
Mr. D. Simpson, B.Sc. M.B., Ch.B.

TRAINERS: G. A. Williams; W. McArthur   **ASSISTANT SECRETARY:** R. A. Moules.
COACHES: F. G. L. Ford; J. Crawford.

EASTVILLE STADIUM · BRISTOL

59

David Pegg.   **Dennis Viollet.**

United's preparations were not exactly what they would have wanted. Duncan Edwards pulled out with a septic knee, while Johnny Berry did not leave Manchester with his teammates due to a family illness, travelling alone and not reaching the team hotel until after midnight. Eddie Colman was also a late arrival from his army camp at Catterick, reaching Bristol around 10pm on the Friday night.

A couple of early Rovers attacks were comfortably dealt with by the United defence, who relieved the immediate danger by passing the ball back to Ray Wood in the United goal. At the opposite end United's first serious attack, which saw Berry and Taylor force their way down the right, ended with Rovers' 'keeper, Nicholls, pulling off an excellent save from Taylor after the United centre-forward cut inside and shot from a narrow angle.

The 20-year-old Nicholls, who had only made his Bristol Rovers debut the previous week, showed no signs of nerves against his illustrious opponents, and his clearance from Taylor's shot saw his teammates converge on the United goal. Amid a rather desperate melee, Foulkes managed to clear the danger.

Pegg managed to get a good cross in towards the Rovers' goal, but it was to finds its way over to the opposite side to be gathered by Johnny Berry. It was then lobbed back into the goalmouth where Viollet, only six yards out, managed to head it wide of the post when it looked odds-on that he would have scored.

It would prove to be a costly miss, as a minute later Bristol Rovers took the lead. Following some rather scrappy play in midfield, the ball broke to Petherbridge, who immediately crossed it into the United goalmouth. Here, it bounced off one of the many bodies in the area and fell nicely for Biggs, who hit it first time past the unsighted Wood and into the far corner of the net.

With only 10 minutes gone, United found themselves behind, with the home side certainly playing the better football, allowing the visitors little time to settle on the ball. Berry was twice bundled rather unceremoniously off the ball, but neither of the free-kicks came to anything and play was soon back in the United half of the field.

Wood was thankfully on hand to save a header from Biggs as his fellow defenders waited for an offside decision that never materialised, but the raised flag of a linesman for offside did defuse a certain goal after Whitefoot had lost the ball in midfield and Petherbridge moved towards Wood with the goal at his mercy.

A couple of chances did come United's way, but Pegg's centre was too far forward for anyone to get on the end off, while from the opposite flank Berry sent a 12-yard drive across the face of the Rovers' goal, with no one near to nudge it in.

With the home forward line all over six-feet tall they were winning all the aerial battles, but one high ball into the United area saw both Foulkes and Wood go for it. Wood failed to clear it, and it bounced towards Hooper, who spotted Biggs unmarked in front of goal. Fortunately for United the Rovers' inside-forward scooped the ball over the bar as the goal stood wide open.

Biggs, a constant threat to the visitors, also came close with an overhead kick from around 15 yards out, but it went narrowly over, much to the relief of Wood.

United thought they had drawn level in the 32nd minute when they won a free-kick just outside the area for a foul by Pitt on Pegg. Taken by Byrne, he slammed the ball into the Rovers' net but was disappointed when the referee signalled for a goal-kick, telling the frustrated United captain that the kick had been indirect.

Jones was booked for a foul on Petherbridge after the Rovers' outside-right had got the better of Byrne, and the resulting free-kick caused a goalmouth scramble, and a header from Bradford was cleared off the goalline at the expense of corner-kick.

With only a minute remaining until the interval, United went two down. A long pass from Allcock found Bradford on the left, who then switched play to the opposite side, and Petherbridge beat Byrne on the inside before sending in a low centre. This should have been cleared but instead fell to Meyer, who missed with his first attempt but made no mistake with his second, which he hit firmly past Wood.

Rovers almost struck again immediately after the interval, with United reduced to 10 men. Mark Jones was nowhere to be seen and only quick thinking by Wood kept United in the game. They were quickly back at full strength upon the centre-half's return, however, and they moved towards the home goal. Taylor ghosted past Allcock, and from his cross a goalmouth scramble ensued before Nicholls managed to save. The Bristol 'keeper had to be at his best again when his defence was under pressure, this time saving on the goalline from David Pegg.

Despite its experience the United defence was finding it difficult to keep the Rovers' forward line under control, while upfront their own forward line was also lacking in their usual composure. Winning a free-kick, they failed to turn it into a scoring opportunity, and from the clearance Bristol Rovers were once again on the attack.

Bradford chased the long, hopeful ball down the left and, upon gaining possession, lobbed it into the United goalmouth. Whitefoot hesitated and lost the ball to Biggs, who moved in on goal, and as Wood came out to narrow the angle the Rovers' inside-right steered the ball past him into the net.

With just under half an hour remaining United were struggling to put passes together, never mind score, and looked to be on their way out of the FA Cup.

Biggs and Bradford both came close to adding to the Rovers' total with headers that went narrowly over the bar, and the team as a whole now had something of a shoot-on-sight mentality, keeping Wood on his toes. He made three excellent saves in quick concession to keep the scoring down.

Byrne had to head off the line from Meyer as the ball continued to remain in and around the United goal, and from another corner in the 83rd minute Bradford's header beat Wood, but Byrne dived and pushed it round the post with his hand. From the resulting penalty Bradford simply stood over the ball and, without any run up, hit it past Wood. United were now dead and buried, and for the remainder of the game they more or less gave up.

Why had United failed so miserably against Bristol Rovers? Tom Jackson of the *Manchester Evening News* felt that such a result was 'bound to happen,' and he wrote that it raised the question of 'whether the Busby youngsters need an "old head" to guide them on the field – a team general to rally them when things are going wrong'. Jackson, however, didn't go along with the argument and suggested that 'although the Cup defeat was disappointing, it should make no difference to the club policy of grooming and developing young players – a policy that has already stamped itself on United's general team pattern and that promises greater things for the future'. He also added, 'And who will deny that in the years ahead United may have another outstanding team "general" in Duncan Edwards, whose absence from the Cup tie at Bristol was such a big blow.'

United's FA Cup fortune changed for the better in both of the following seasons, but as the 1950s drew to a close and a new decade got under way there were further embarrassing moments along the Wembley trail, and it wasn't until the trophy was eventually won in 1963 that the 15-year wait finally came to an end.

Bristol Rovers: Nicholls, Bamford, Allcock, Pitt, Hale, Sampson, Petherbridge, Biggs, Bradford, Meyer, Hooper.
Scorers: Biggs 2, Meyer, Bradford.
Manchester United: Wood, Foulkes, Byrne, Colman, Jones, Whitefoot, Berry, Doherty, Taylor, Viollet, Pegg.
Attendance: 22,216.

No. 11
UNITED V BLACKPOOL
7 April 1956

Despite home and away victories over Chelsea during the Stamford Bridge side's title-winning season of 1954–55, United were still not thought of as automatic heirs to the Championship crown for the following season.

Having finished fifth, with some indifferent displays along the way, there was still work to be done, and although with the youthful resources within his grasp, exciting young players who attracted thousands to their FA Youth Cup and Central League fixtures, Matt Busby still had some fine-tuning to apply to his team to take them to the pinnacle of the English game.

As season 1955–56 got under way it was with some disappointment that the opening two fixtures, against Birmingham City away and Tottenham Hotspur at home, ended in 2–2 draws, but with the other two August fixtures bringing victories, 3–1 against West Bromwich Albion at Old Trafford and 2–1 at White Hart Lane, it was thought that the show was at last on the road.

Everyone was, however, brought back down to earth with a bang as Manchester City triumphed 1–0 in the first derby of the season, while consecutive defeats against Sheffield United (1–0) and Everton (4–2), who they had beaten 2–1 seven days earlier, kept United two points behind early leaders Blackpool, with the Seasiders having played a game less.

As October brought the darker nights, it also brought an upsurge in the performances of Busby's team, with 15 goals scored in the five pre-Halloween fixtures, including four in the pulsating 90 minutes against Wolves and Aston Villa. However, despite only managing to defeat Cardiff City 1–0 at Ninian Park, it was enough to see United skip over new leaders Sunderland into top spot, even if they had to surrender the position a couple of weeks later.

A glance at the Central League table from the same time shows United's second string also ruling the roost, two points in front of Liverpool with a game in hand, giving Busby some relief should any of his first-choice players suffer injuries.

United's visit to Bloomfield Road on 26 November to face a Blackpool side who were once again sitting at the top of the tree, having slipped off the top spot only twice since the opening day, was too early in the season to have any say on the actual destination of the title, but the points could give either side a little bit of breathing space. As it turned out neither team gained any advantage, with the game ending 1–1, and it was considered by the 26-odd thousand who were present to be something of a disappointment.

A 2–1 victory over Sunderland the following Saturday, while Blackpool only drew at Tottenham, saw United return to the top, but the positions changed again seven days later when

Last League Match

UNITED

v.

PORTSMOUTH

Saturday, 21st April

Kick off 3 p.m.

United lost 3–2 at Portsmouth and Everton were thumped 4–0 as the Christmas lights were taking the place of the famous Illuminations along the Golden Mile.

The following week the two Lancashire sides once again swapped places as United defeated Birmingham City, and Blackpool, on this occasion, conceded four, losing at Arsenal.

Into 1956 and United held firmly onto that top spot, and by the end of February they had established a six-point lead. Blackpool, however, had a game in hand. But if Matt Busby and his players needed something of a jolt to keep their minds firmly focused on the job and not to take anything for granted, it came on Saturday 24 March, with United five points clear, although still having played a game more than Blackpool.

With United facing Bolton Wanderers at Old Trafford, many of the 40-odd thousand in the ground took more than a passing interest in events down the East Lancs Road at Aintree, where the Grand National was taking place. Coming up to the final fence, the Queen Mother's horse, Devon Loch, was in front and looking a certain winner. Having cleared the fence, it stumbled on the flat and fell, allowing the second-placed horse to gallop past and on to victory. Would United suffer a similar mishap?

United managed to overcome Bolton by a solitary goal, while Blackpool beat Birmingham City, but seven days later the Seasiders slipped up at home to Sheffield United, only managing a point in a 1–1 draw. There were now only half a dozen games remaining, and one of those was almost certainly the one that was going to be the title decider – Blackpool's visit to Manchester on 7 April.

Wins against Newcastle United and Huddersfield kept United within touching distance of that Championship trophy, and on Easter Monday a victory over Newcastle United at St James Park would have secured the title. As it turned out, the celebrations were put on hold as United failed to score for the first time in 15 League games and had to be content with a point from the 0–0 draw.

On the afternoon of 7 April Blackpool left the Tower, Pleasure Beach and Golden Mile and headed for Manchester. Whether they consulted any of the gypsy fortune tellers along the promenade prior to leaving is unrecorded, but even if they had crossed their palms with silver, they would also have had to call upon some sort of spell being cast upon their opponents if they were going to somehow snatch the title from United's grasp.

There were still six points between the two sides, but Blackpool had four games to play while United only had three, so it was something of a tall order to expect United, even if they did lose to Blackpool, to also fail against Sunderland and Portsmouth in the final two fixtures.

Strangely, Matt Busby had taken his team to Blackpool for a couple of days training prior to the game, and they returned on the day of the match to find the area around Old Trafford overflowing with people and vehicles. Such was the congestion that the gates, which had been ordered to open two hours prior to kick-off, were firmly shut 15 minutes prior to the start with just over 60,000 packed inside, the ground's biggest post-war crowd. Busby, however, was not present, having had to travel north due to a family bereavement.

With squads of policemen, some mounted, attempting to bring some sort of order to the vast number of supporters locked outside Old Trafford, many were still debating whether to make their way back home, go to the nearest public house, or to simply remain at the ground, listening to the noise emanating from behind the red brick walls when the drama of the afternoon began to unfold.

United, unbeaten at home all season, found themselves a goal behind with only two minutes played. Blackpool's live duck mascot, accompanied by his 'eastern prince' had certainly brought some luck with them from the Lancashire resort, with the aforementioned fortune tellers perhaps performing some underhand tactics to ensure a Blackpool victory.

Attacking from the outset, Blackpool immediately put the home defence under pressure, and Jones was forced to head clear when Ernie Taylor sent a high ball forward towards Mudie. Edwards was then called upon to clear another attack but in the process was forced to give away a throw-in. From the throw Matthews found Mudie, who immediately turned the ball inside to Durie, running in practically unmarked to head firmly past Wood.

The Blackpool support went wild with delight, thinking that there was indeed a possibility of pulling off the supposedly impossible.

United, attacking the Stretford End, had different ideas and came close to an equaliser twice in as many minutes. Taylor worked the ball through to Viollet, but his right-footed shot not only beat Farm in the Blackpool goal but also flashed past the far post. Then it was Edwards, latching on to a Berry free-kick with a powerful drive from about 30 yards out, which was deflected out to Doherty. The United inside-forward headed the ball back towards goal, and although Farm was once again beaten he was relieved to see the ball hit the crossbar before being cleared by a teammate to safety.

Matthews was doing his utmost to ensure that the chances of obtaining a League Championship medal remained a distinct possibility, and he constantly switched wings, keeping the United defence on their toes. Attacking from the left, his cross eluded Wood, but fortunately Byrne was on hand to head behind for a corner.

There was a hint of nerves among the United players, but thankfully Roger Byrne remained calm under pressure, nipping a Taylor-Matthews move before it could cause any real danger. He was also quick to offer support to his forwards, and with around 20 minutes played his cross into the Blackpool goalmouth should have resulted in the equaliser. Falling invitingly, it just required the simplest of flicks from Viollet, who was completely unmarked a couple of yards out, but he jumped a fraction too soon and the opportunity was lost.

Six minutes later it once again looked as though the equaliser was about to materialise when Berry turned the ball in towards the Blackpool goal. Doherty got his head firmly behind it, and it went past the outstretched hand of Farm only for Frith to head clear from underneath the crossbar.

Soon afterwards it was again the turn of the usually dependable Viollet to surrender the chance of the equaliser. Tommy Taylor's cross beat Gratrix and Kelly, and Viollet tried to place his shot past Farm, but the goalkeeper managed to divert the effort wide with his legs.

It was now United who were enjoying most of the play, but still that equalising goal would not materialise. Doherty saw a shot flash across the Blackpool goal and then had another effort blocked by Farm. Then, with only minutes of the first half remaining, Berry forced the ball into the Blackpool area, and from Viollet's pass Taylor's goal-bound effort was once again cleared off the line by Frith.

With United still a goal behind, they started the second half as they finished the first. Taylor was foiled by Gratrix and Pegg shot over the top of what was more or less an empty goal before one of his cross-field passes was missed by everyone. Taylor, injured for the second time in a matter of minutes, this time following a collision with Wright, had to leave the field with a cut head, but it was while both players were off the pitch receiving attention that United scored the equaliser.

Berry, having moved into the middle, sent Doherty racing through on goal, but just as he was about to shoot, Farm came racing out of his goal and bundled the United man over before scrambling the ball away. The referee had no hesitation in pointing to the penalty spot and, to everyone's surprise, Roger Byrne, the usual penalty taker, allowed Johnny Berry to take the kick. The winger blasted the ball past Farm to equalise.

Doherty appeared to lose some of his effectiveness with a slight injury, while the visitors also found themselves in a similar situation with Durie and also Wright, who had been injured in the earlier clash with Taylor. The game, however, continued to move from end to end as Blackpool fought to keep their faint hopes alive and United battled for the Championship crown.

The visitors, to their credit, kept the United defence occupied but always seemed to be outnumbered at the last vital moment. With 10 minutes remaining the Seasiders knew that their luck had finally run out when Berry directed a pass right to the feet of Tommy Taylor, standing only a few feet away from goal, and the United centre-forward beat Farm with ease. Frith, having twice rescued his side with goalline clearances, was once again situated behind his goalkeeper and got a hand to the ball, but he could not stop it from going over the line. The referee, with the decision to make as to a goal or a penalty, gave the former, and United were at last in front.

Berry, who had enjoyed one of his best games for the club, certainly out-dazzling the incomparable Matthews, was relieved that the referee had decided to award the goal as he later said, 'I hadn't the strength to take another penalty by that time.'

Taylor almost added a third but could only watch as his shot beat Farm, only for Gratrix to head over the bar.

The noise that greeted the final whistle was deafening as players and supporters alike celebrated. 'I can hardly realise the Championship trophy is ours at last and that the months of tension since we took the lead last December are over,' said United captain Roger Byrne. 'Blackpool were worthy opponents. We never underrated their challenge and could not take anything for granted. But we United players were not only fighting for the title today. We were all pulling out our best for the man who has done all the scheming and worrying for us – our manager, Mr Busby. What a pity he couldn't be with us to share this hour of triumph.'

Matt Busby was informed of the victory when he stopped and telephoned the ground as he made his way back from Scotland, but he had not missed the presentation of the League Championship trophy as that did not take place until after the final fixture of the season against Portsmouth, which, rather surprisingly, only attracted a crowd of 38,417. It wasn't the lowest of the campaign by a long shot, as there were a few even below 30,000, including the visit of the reigning champions, Chelsea, which could only bring 22,192 through the turnstiles.

A minute and a half before the end of the Portsmouth game, thousands poured over the fencing, surrounding the pitch as the referee's whistle blew, but it was a premature celebration as the official was only signalling a free-kick. However, it was soon officially over and the crowd once again surged forward towards the mouth of the tunnel, intent on obtaining a better view of Roger Byrne receiving the Championship trophy from Mr Joe Richards of the Football League Management Committee.

Matt Busby had at last succeeded not only in rebuilding his aging side but in guiding them to the pinnacle of the English game. It was, however, only the beginning.

Manchester United: Wood, Greaves, Byrne, Colman, Jones, Edwards, Berry, Doherty, T. Taylor, Viollet, Pegg.
Scorers: Berry (penalty), Taylor.
Blackpool: Farm, Frith, Wright, J. Kelly, Gratrix, H. Kelly, Matthews, E. Taylor, Mudie, Durie, Perry.
Scorer: Durie.
Attendance: 62,277.

No. 12
UNITED V ANDERLECHT
26 September 1956

With football clubs not only in Britain but also across Europe always seeking to better themselves, matches against teams from outside their own country provided such opportunities while also proving to be extremely popular with supporters. After much thought, Gabriel Hanot, a French sports journalist and editor of the much-respected publication *L'Equipe*, suggested that the clubs who finished top of their domestic Leagues should compete against each other for a European Cup. Sixteen clubs competed in the inaugural 1955–56 competition, but First Division champions Chelsea were refused permission to take part by the Football League.

As First Division champions for 1955–56, Matt Busby was more than eager for his team to take part in the European Cup as he sensed that, no matter what the results brought, the actual experience would be priceless. These sentiments were echoed by Sir Stanley Rous, secretary of the Football Association, and with the 1955–56 season only just finished he sent the following letter, dated 14 May, to Walter Crickmer, the United secretary:

'You will no doubt have heard of the European Champions Clubs' Cup competition in which last season Hibernians took part and Chelsea F.C. withdrew. The final of this competition will be played on June 13th in Paris between Real Madrid and Reims.

'The Committee of the Competition is most anxious that for this coming season all the champions of the various countries in Europe should take part, and they ask whether your club would consider entering the competition.

'The financial advantages are many and the competition is run on the usual Cup system. Each team will meet the same opponents twice, on the home and away basis. The clubs are paired by drawing of lots.

'I enclose herewith the Regulations of the Competition and I should be grateful if you would study them and let me know whether your club intends to take part. I should be grateful for an early reply as the European Union should be notified before May 20th.

'All the matches in the competition are mutually arranged between the clubs concerned on dates which are convenient to both. Last year Hibernians were called upon to play six matches and were knocked out in the semi-final tie by Reims: their

matches were all played on mid-week dates, which fitted in quite conveniently with their League programme.

'I think this could be an excellent opportunity for your club and should show a good financial return.'

Busby needed little encouragement and had already spoken to his directors regarding participating in the competition, so when the invitation came through the Old Trafford letter box it was immediately accepted. It wasn't, however, simply a case of RSVP and turn up wherever the draw took you because permission had to be given by the Football League and, as Chelsea had already found to their disappointment, the powers that be were not exactly accommodating. Busby, certainly not put off by Chelsea's failure, informed his board that he wanted to take part and they should write and ask the Football League for permission to do so.

In the summer of 1956 a letter requesting the League's permission was sent off and a reply eagerly awaited back in Manchester. When it finally did arrive, dated 21 August, it did not go down well with the United directors and certainly not with Matt Busby. It read:

'The Management Committee have considered your letters with regard to your entry into this competition and they quite understand that you entered the competition in good faith. Nevertheless I am instructed to write you as follows :-

'The Management Committee consider that participation in such a competition is not in the best interests of the League as a whole, clashing as it does with the League competition. They therefore ask you to reconsider your decision to participate in the light of its possible effect on attendances at League matches when you are playing at home.'

United wasted little time in replying, and three days later Walter Crickmer popped it in the post to the Football League at their Preston headquarters, with the message getting straight to the point.

'Your letter, reference FH/JB, of the 21st instent (sic), was submitted to my directors at their meeting last evening.

'My board very much regret that at this late date it is impossible to withdraw from the above competition. All arrangements have been made for the home and away games v Anderlecht, tickets have been printed, and the applications are now being dealt with.

'My directors are pleased to note the Management Committee realise that we entered the competition in good faith, and notwithstanding that the existing rule does not call for any payment to the Football League from the receipts of matches in the competition, my board instruct me to say that they will in any event make the usual payment of 4% to the League so long as our interest in the competition continues.'

71

Forceful and to the point, with a hint of bribery, it was enough to ensure United's participation in the 1956–57 European Cup, thus beginning their sojourn into European football and what, over the years, was to become something of a roller coaster ride, bringing triumphs and tears as well as countless never-to-be-forgotten memories.

So it was off to Belgium for the first leg of the opening round of the competition, and Matt Busby could not have wished for a better performance with which to open Manchester United's European account.

Dennis Viollet gave United the lead in the 25th minute with an exceptional effort. Having repelled an Anderlecht attack, Mark Jones cleared the ball towards the diminutive Eddie Colman, who in turn pushed it forward to Viollet, who was positioned just over the halfway line. Gathering the ball in his stride, Viollet set off for goal, and having evaded the attention of de Koster, the Anderlecht centre-half, he let fly with a powerful left-footed drive from six yards out, which gave Week in the Anderlecht goal no chance whatsoever.

It is interesting to note that special permission for leave – between 12 noon on Monday 10 September and 12 noon on Friday 14 September – had to be sought from Major Pounds of the Royal Signals in Richmond to enable 23149671 Sig Eddie Colman to travel and play in Belgium.

United continued to keep the home side at bay, and 15 minutes from the end they claimed a two-goal advantage when Viollet created the opportunity for Taylor to head home in typical fashion.

The scoreline, however, could have taken on a totally different perspective if Lippers, the Anderlecht right-half, had scored from the penalty spot just after half-time. His spot-kick hit the post and rebounded to the feet of teammate Gaston de Wael, but the centre-forward's effort was brilliantly saved by United 'keeper Ray Wood.

United took a 2–0 advantage back to Manchester, but they were well aware that the tie wasn't over, although Anderlecht had shown little appetite for European football, having lost to MTK Budapest 10–4 on aggregate in the first round of the previous season's inaugural competition. By the end of the second leg, under the Maine Road lights, the Belgians were more than grateful that their journey home was not an overly long one.

The lack of floodlights at Old Trafford was certainly something that had to be overcome if United were going to participate in the European Cup, but having shared Manchester City's Maine Road ground during those immediate post-war seasons, there was little concern as to whether their local rivals would refuse a request for the use of their ground for however many games United's Cup campaign would last. In any case, plans for installing floodlights at Old Trafford were at an advanced stage.

City would also gain from hosting such fixtures, as a letter between the two clubs, dated 13 August 1956, confirmed that their directors 'will be pleased to loan you Maine Road ground on 26th September for your European Cup tie on terms of £300 or 15% of the net gate, whichever is the greater.'

On the night, the playing conditions at Maine Road were far from ideal due to persistent heavy rain, which also kept the attendance down to just over 40,000, probably much to City's regret, with pools of surface water obvious in areas across the pitch. Although those conditions were the same for both sides, the Belgians appeared to slip and slide across the muddy pitch in their rather fruitless attempt to subdue the tide of red shirts that moved constantly towards them.

The 90 minutes almost started badly for United. Straight from the kick-off Mermans pushed the ball through towards his inside-left, Derwael, but due to the conditions it slipped across the surface and became marooned in a pool of water, and the opportunity was gone.

With eight minutes passed, David Pegg, for whom the conditions caused few, if any, problems, and who gave Anderlecht full-back Gettenmans a torrid time, created the opening goal when he centred the ball for Taylor to head home. The United centre-forward claimed his second of the night 13 minutes later with a left-footed drive, with Pegg once again the provider.

Anderlecht had no answer to United's quick, forceful, attacking play, and if Taylor had been an early thorn in Anderlecht's side then they were even more sickened by the sight of Dennis Viollet moving towards goal as Taylor's left-sided partner claimed a hat-trick within the space of 13 minutes.

Viollet's first and United's third came in the 27th minute when he moved onto a long ball down the middle. He dribbled round full-back Culot and goalkeeper Week and slipped the ball into the net. Six minutes later he seized upon a mis-timed pass back by Culot, quickly nipping in to score his second, latching onto the ball as his initial attempt rebounded off the post. With five minutes remaining before the interval, a Berry centre, following an across-field move between Whelan, Taylor and Berry, enabled Viollet to notch his hat-trick.

The Belgians were now on the ropes and would have been more than happy for the referee to call a premature end to the contest, but United were far from finished. Within three minutes of the second half getting under way it was 6–0, Tommy Taylor staking his claim for the match ball, pouncing as the Anderlecht goalkeeper dropped a Whelan cross.

The visitors had not shown much of a challenge from the outset, but they were now sunk without trace and were

Eddie Colman.

completely lost and bewildered as to what they should try in an attempt to keep the scoreline from increasing further. United, on the other hand, showed little mercy and made no attempt to ease off, continuing to attack from all angles and at every possible opportunity. Jones was solid at the back, giving Mermans little space, while Colman was first to every ball in midfield.

Week picked the ball out of his net for a seventh time in the 64th minute, after Liam Whelan got in on the goalscoring act, following good work down the right from Byrne and Berry, slipping the ball into an empty net as the Belgian 'keeper lay floundering in the Maine Road mud, unable to offer any resistance.

The Belgian goalkeeper, however, was not as incompetent as the scoreline suggested and, upon reflection, United could certainly have scored more had it not been for a handful of outstanding saves. His centre-half, Dekoster, also played his part in keeping the scoreline from being even more embarrassing than it actually was.

Dennis Viollet made it 8–0 11 minutes later as the onslaught continued and, following several near misses, Johnny Berry made it nine in the 85th minute.

Despite the scoreline and United's overwhelming superiority, few people left the ground as they wanted to savour every possible minute of an attacking display superior to anything that they had previously witnessed and which they would quite probably never see again, and they were certainly correct in their decision. With three minutes remaining Whelan claimed a second as the harassed Belgian defence surrendered to yet another superb United attacking move, and as he turned away after scoring, the Irishman looked slightly apologetic.

Humiliated and completely annihilated, the Anderlecht players did not trudge off the pitch heads down when the referee's whistle signalled full time. Instead, as the crowd gave United a standing ovation, they clapped their conquerors from the pitch in true sportsman-like fashion.

No one from the Football League had cared to travel to Manchester for a momentous occasion in English football, but Matt Busby's side had certainly justified their manager's decision to enter the competition, although judging from the two legs against Anderlecht it would be the opposition who would be learning from United rather than the other way about.

'I can never hope in the rest of a lifetime to see anything better than this,' said Matt Busby at the end. Little did the United manager know that in the months and years ahead he was going to be proved wrong.

Manchester United: Wood, Foulkes, Byrne, Colman, Jones, Edwards, Berry, Whelan, Taylor, Viollet, Pegg.
Scorers: Viollet 4, Taylor 3, Whelan 2, Berry.
Anderlecht: Week, Gettemans, Culot, Van Der Wilt, de Koster, Hannon, Dedridver, Vandendosch, Mermans, Derwael, Jurion.
Attendance: 43,635.

No. 13

UNITED V CHARLTON ATHLETIC
6 October 1956

There are a few teams scattered through this volume of memorable matches that one would certainly not associate with classic encounters, with Bristol Rovers, Hartlepools United, Norwich City and Huddersfield Town among them. Another of these is Charlton Athletic, a club that feature regularly in the history of Manchester United, and one of its players in particular.

It may surprise many to read that Charlton Athletic were a regular feature in the First Division in the immediate post-war period, but seldom did they enjoy favourable results against United. Indeed, their only victories between the resumption of League football in season 1946–47 and their visit to Old Trafford in October 1956 were the 1–0 home victory in April 1954 and the rather surprising 3–0 victory, also at The Valley, in December 1956, 24 hours after having been beaten 5–1 at Old Trafford. They could also claim the distinction of being the last London club to leave Old Trafford with a victory.

On an interesting note, prior to the outbreak of war in 1940, United's last Football League fixture (only three had been completed) was against Charlton Athletic at The Valley, where they lost 2–0 in front of a mere 8,608 spectators.

When Charlton Athletic journeyed north in early October 1956 they were languishing joint-bottom of the First Division, with only five points from their 10 games, having conceded 21 goals and scored 14. They were also looking for their first away points of the season. Conversely, United were riding the crest of the wave, sitting in top spot, some 13 points in front of their visitors.

In the 1950s and indeed the 1960s, if a club was honoured by the selection of one or even more of its players for international duty, it could not hope for a postponement of a domestic fixture if it happened to fall on the same day as the international just because its star player or players were missing. It simply had to get on with it and hope that the replacements were slightly more than adequate.

This was the position that Matt Busby found himself in back in October 1956, as on the same day that United were playing Charlton Athletic at Old Trafford, England were due to face Northern Ireland at Windsor Park, Belfast, with the selectors of both countries calling on United players. In the Irish 11 was the versatile Jackie Blanchflower, while England laid claim to Roger Byrne, Duncan Edwards and Tommy Taylor, leaving Busby with something of a patching-up job at a time when there was no squad system, with your first 11 being

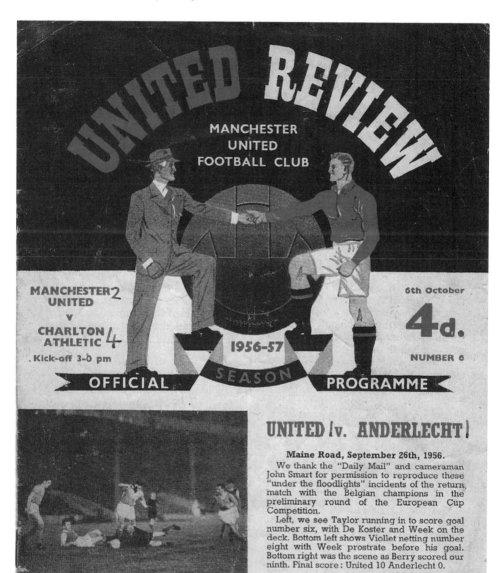

UNITED [v. ANDERLECHT]

Maine Road, September 26th, 1956.

We thank the "Daily Mail" and cameraman John Smart for permission to reproduce these "under the floodlights" incidents of the return match with the Belgian champions in the preliminary round of the European Cup Competition.

Left, we see Taylor running in to score goal number six, with De Koster and Week on the deck. Bottom left shows Viollet netting number eight with Week prostrate before his goal. Bottom right was the scene as Berry scored our ninth. Final score : United 10 Anderlecht 0.

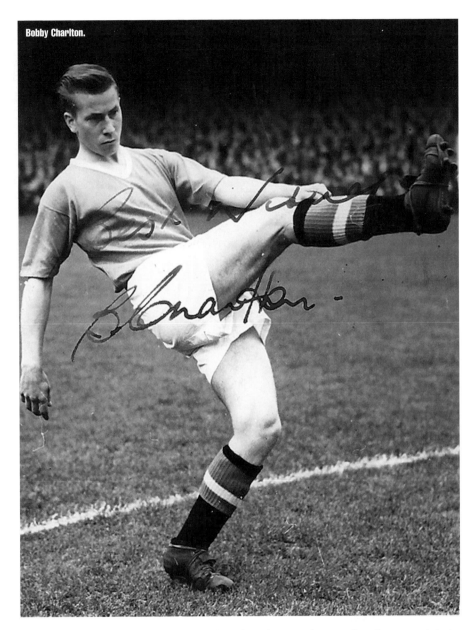

Bobby Charlton.

exactly what it said and automatically selected week in, week out unless there were injuries or occasions such as this.

The United manager had to delve into his Central League side for replacements, a side that sat eighth in their League and what had been defeated 7–1 the week before by 'The Rest', a select 11 from the best of the other Central League clubs. But it was a team that did not lack experience, as Busby could call upon the likes of Geoff Bent and Wilf McGuinness to replace Byrne and Edwards. Although they were both making their first appearances of the season, full-back Bent had made his League debut back in season 1954–55, while McGuinness had made his initial appearance in the previous season.

Jackie Blanchflower had yet to feature in Busby's first-team selections of this campaign, so no actual replacement was required, but replacing Tommy Taylor saw Busby introduce 18-year-old Ashington-born Bobby Charlton for his first-team debut.

Charlton had joined United straight from school on amateur forms in January 1953 after winning England Schoolboy honours, and he soon became an influential part of United's successful and hugely talented youth team, which monopolised the FA Youth Cup for its first five years. Playing in the 1954, 1955 and 1956 Finals alongside other talented youngsters such as Duncan Edwards, Eddie Colman, David Pegg, Wilf McGuinness, Alex Dawson, Shay Brennan and Kenny Morgans, it wasn't long before the name of Bobby Charlton was being spoken of as 'one for the future'.

The player himself was later to recall, 'I was scoring goals and everybody kept saying "You'll be in the first team soon." But I looked at them and thought, "How am I going to get in?" I was an attacking inside or centre-forward, and we had Tommy Taylor, Dennis Viollet, Billy Whelan, John Doherty and Colin Webster.'

When his opportunity finally came due to the international call-up for Tommy Taylor, he almost missed it. 'Three weeks before, I'd been injured at Maine Road in a reserve match. I twisted my ligaments in my right ankle and it took me two weeks to start running again. During the week of the Charlton game, Matt Busby asked, "How's your ankle?" and as I knew this was my chance, I replied "Fine". It was as sore as hell, not when I ran, but when I turned on it or tried to kick the ball. But I knew I had to get in. I was desperate.'

In Charlton went, but it was Charlton Athletic who shone in the opening minutes, almost scoring within 20 seconds. Moving down the United left, Ayre hit an excellent ball into the United area directly to the feet of Leary. It looked as if the centre-forward could not miss as he sent the ball goalwards, but Ray Wood somehow managed to push the ball round the post for a corner.

Play soon switched to the opposite end. Pegg was fouled 25 yards out, and from the resulting free-kick Viollet saw his flick go fractionally wide of the post. Another effort, this time from Charlton centre-half Hewie, almost led to an own-goal as the Scottish international nearly sliced a Berry centre past his own 'keeper. Fortunately for him the ball went out for a corner.

Berry, captaining the side in place of Roger Byrne, was thriving in the responsibility and was a constant threat to the Charlton defence. He was unfortunate to see a goal-bound shot strike left-back Ellis and go wide for a corner.

Despite efforts from Pegg, who was fractionally late in getting to Viollet's cross, and Whelan, who watched in despair as his header went narrowly wide of the post, the visitors were playing well and certainly did not look like a team who were propping up the table as they kept Foulkes, Bent and Jones on their toes, continuing to push forward at every opportunity.

Indeed, it was Charlton who went in front in the 24th minute when the ball was cleared out of their defence down the centre of the park by Ellis. Jones managed to head the ball away, but it only went as far as Gauld, who slipped it wide to Lucas, and the inside-left hit the ball along the ground and into the corner of the net.

It was a lead that Charlton held for only 60 seconds, however. Berry, having moved inside, controlled the ball and drove it through a crowd of players and into the net for the equaliser. A second might well have followed a few minutes later when Berry's centre was headed weakly into the hands of Marsh, the Charlton 'keeper, when Berry really should have done better, especially as Charlton was waiting in front of goal for the pass that never came.

On the half-hour mark United did take the lead. Bent cleared the ball forward and it was collected by Bobby Charlton, who, taking the ball in his stride, beat a couple of defenders with ease before shooting along the ground from around 25 yards out and into the far corner.

Six minutes later Bobby had notched his second. Colman and Pegg started the move, which saw Viollet swing the ball out to the left, where the debutant was completely unmarked. Controlling the ball with his chest, he calmly drove it wide of the Charlton 'keeper.

It now looked as if United would go on to add to their total, but the visitors surprised them by fighting back and equalising within two minutes. Colman, holding onto the ball for too long, lost possession, and White set the decisive move in motion. Quickly switching the ball from left to right, he found Ayre, the outside-right, who volleyed the ball towards the United goal and into the net, giving Wood no chance whatsoever.

With half-time beckoning, Bobby Charlton shunned the chance of his hat-trick, missing an opportunity that was even easier to accept than those of the two he had scored. Standing only a matter of six yards out, he somehow managed to hook the ball over the cross-bar when more or less underneath it.

Early in the second half Charlton were fortunate not to concede a penalty. O'Linn appeared to jump at the feet of Whelan, and when the referee blew his whistle everyone thought that it was for a penalty, but rather surprisingly the official awarded an indirect free-kick, which came to nothing.

Despite enjoying most of the play, United simply could not turn their fine passing movements into goals, often playing one pass too many. Viollet came close to adding a third, but his right-footed shot, following good work between Pegg and Charlton, was well held by Marsh. Moments later the United player was being spoken to by the referee following an incident with O'Linn.

From the resulting free-kick, Campbell shot over, and on the hour the United defence were almost caught out when Lucas got round Jones and then proceeded to walk round the advancing Wood. Thinking he had nothing more to do than touch the ball into the empty net, Lucas was surprised when Foulkes appeared, as if from nowhere, to clear off the line at the expense of a corner.

With 25 minutes remaining and just when it looked as though Charlton were going to get back into the game, United made it 4–2. The ball was pushed out to David Pegg, whose cross found Whelan in front of goal. The young Irishman's shot was blocked by Marsh, but the 'keeper was unable to hold the ball and, regaining possession, Whelan blasted the ball home.

It was an important goal as not only did it give United the breathing space they needed to see out the remainder of the game, it kept them within touching distance of breaking Burnley's record of 30 League games unbeaten, which had stood since season 1920–21. They had played some 25 games without losing.

Hewie had to clear twice as United pushed forward, while Viollet continued to impress, covering most of the pitch in search of the ball. Pegg almost added a fifth, but Marsh saved well to keep the scoreline down to a respectable level.

In the end United were simply too strong for their visitors, who returned to London empty-handed, having won only two of their dozen games. As for the debutant Bobby Charlton, it was to be simply a case of 'and the rest, as they say, is history'. Despite being unable to hold down a regular first-team place, he did manage a further 13 League appearances during season 1956–57, scoring another eight goals.

Charlton was soon to become one of the first names pencilled onto the team sheet by Matt Busby, and as time progressed he went on to lift almost every honour in the game before retiring at the end of season 1972–73. Following a brief fling in management with Preston North End, as well as having a player-manager role at Deepdale, he made appearances with Waterford before becoming a director with Wigan Athletic, where he also had a spell as caretaker manager.

Bobby Charlton returned to Old Trafford in June 1984 as a director, a position he still holds today.

Manchester United: Wood, Foulkes, Bent, Colman, Jones, McGuinness, Berry, Whelan, Charlton, Viollet, Pegg.
Scorers: Charlton 2, Berry, Whelan.
Charlton Athletic: Marsh, Campbell, Ellis, O'Linn, Hewie, Hammond, Ayre, Gauld, Leary, Lucas, White.
Scorers: Lucas, Ayre.
Attendance: 41,439.

No. 14

MANCHESTER CITY V UNITED
24 October 1956

No listing of memorable United games would be complete without an encounter against our neighbours from across the city. The only problem this actually creates is which match, or even matches, should be included. There were times, of course, when Manchester City did not share the same fixture list as United, and there was one season in the 70s when the positions were reversed, with the Reds dropping below the Blues to the Second Division for the first time since the war.

Delving through the fixtures from the 1950s in search of at least one 90 minutes of note, we take a closer look at the Maine Road encounter of 24 October 1956, which not only had local pride at stake but also the Charity Shield trophy. This particular mid-week fixture early in the season brought together the FA Cup winners and the First Division champions – a rare occasion in itself.

City had lifted the FA Cup with a 3–1 victory over Birmingham City at Wembley Stadium, having overcome the likes of Blackpool (2–1), Southend United (1–0), Liverpool (2–1, after a 0–0 draw), Everton (2–1) and Tottenham Hotspur in the semi-final (1–0). The 90 minutes under the twin towers is best remembered not for City's success, but for their goalkeeper, Bert Trautmann, showing tremendous bravery – or utter foolishness, depending on how you look at it – by playing for a considerable period of the Final with a broken neck.

United had strode to their fourth First Division Championship in style, finishing 11 points in front of second-placed Blackpool. City has been 14 points behind in fourth.

United had simply strode into season 1956–57 as they had left off a few weeks previously and by early October could be found three points clear of Tottenham Hotspur. City, on the other hand, were in the basement, having already conceded 30 goals, including seven against Arsenal at Highbury.

As Old Trafford awaited the installation of floodlights, United had to relinquish home advantage, returning to the scene of their recent 10–0 victory over Anderlecht in the European Cup. Many hoped for a repeat performance, but this was never going to materialise, although the game, despite the lack of goals, was not without incident.

89

MANCHESTER CITY
FOOTBALL CLUB LTD.

The F. A.
Charity Shield
(Floodlight Match)

MANCHESTER CITY
v.

MANCHESTER UNITED
On Wednesday,
24th October, 1956
KICK-OFF 7-30 p.m.

RESERVED CHAIR 7/6
(Including Tax)

BLOCK B

ROW E

CHAIR No. 177

THIS PORTION TO BE RETAINED

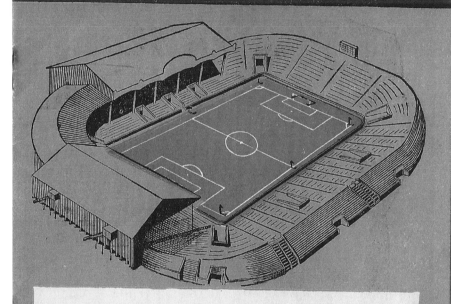

Manchester City
FOOTBALL CLUB LIMITED

WEDNESDAY, 24th OCT., 1956

CHARITY SHIELD

MANCHESTER UNITED

KICK-OFF 7-30 p.m.

MANCHESTER CITY HONOURS LIST

F.A. CUP WINNERS 1904, 1934, 1956
FINALISTS 1926, 1933, 1955

●

LEAGUE CHAMPIONS 1937
RUNNERS-UP 1904, 1921

●

DIVISION II CHAMPIONS 1899,
1903, 1910, 1928, 1947
RUNNERS-UP 1896, 1951

OFFICIAL PROGRAMME · PRICE 3d

The lack of goals was certainly not due to a lack of scoring opportunities, as United certainly had enough to better their triumph over the Belgians, but City put up a courageous, if seldom cohesive, display against their rivals. There were times when they forced Duncan Edwards back into a more defensive role, while Don Revie might have clinched the trophy for the Maine Road boardroom, a victory that would have seen City become the first post-war FA Cup winners to defeat the League Champions in the Charity Shield fixture.

Despite those chances in front of goal, United were far from their best, lacking power, punch and precision, although the little-and-large duo of Eddie Colman and Duncan Edwards in midfield caused City countless problems Their outstanding contribution to the game went unrewarded, however, because once the ball reached the City 18-yard box, the moves suddenly collapsed and evaporated into thin air.

In the *Daily Mail*, Ian Wooldridge wrote, 'Don't get it wrong, this League champions versus Cup-holders clash, a fixture which is a tribute to Manchester's place in English soccer, was entertaining and exciting from start to finish. But at the same time it looked to me like a milestone on United's road back from the supreme to the normal.'

These were strong words indeed, but the game could quite easy have been sewn up in the opening quarter of an hour if not for the uncharacteristic misses from Tommy Taylor, who squandered five ideal scoring opportunities, leaving many wondering as to how he was England's first-choice number nine.

Despite the misses, with Dennis Viollet just as big a culprit as Taylor, the crowd of 30,495, low in numbers due mainly to a combination of the weather and the showing of the game on television, created a superb atmosphere, but they were certainly not rewarded with the goals that they eagerly craved for. However, the game lacked little in excitement.

It wasn't until 17 minutes from the end that the decisive strike materialised. Dennis Viollet,

for once showing his natural talent, slammed the ball past Savage in the City goal. The game, however, hinged around one particular incident – other than the one that ultimately led to that decisive goal – and had City been in better form, then they surely would have capitalised on United's misfortune.

With eight minutes remaining before half-time and City having forced three corners in little more than 60 seconds, United's goalkeeper Ray Wood injured his hip as he attempted to gather the third of those. Unable to continue, Duncan Edwards pulled on the green goalkeeper's jersey and showed his versatility between the posts as half-time beckoned.

Duncan Edwards.

A save by sixteen-year-old David Gaskell, substituting for Ray Wood, injured during the first half of the game.

Edwards' stint as United's last man did not last for long as United were soon back to full strength, with most of those within the stadium and sitting comfortably at home, enjoying the rare event of having live football on the television, presuming that the green-clad figure making his way into the United goalmouth was the injured Wood, having made something of a recovery and resuming his goalkeeping duties.

The spectators couldn't have been more wrong, as the slim-built figure was not the experienced Wood but a Youth-team player by the name of David Gaskell, who had only turned 16 years of age 19 days previously. Substitutes were still something of an unfamiliar feature in the game, hence the presumption that the player was Ray Wood. Even the television commentator failed to note the change. But the appearance of Wigan-born, former England Schoolboy international Gaskell was a story in its own, and one that David revealed when interviewed by the author a number of years ago.

'The real story of my debut has never been told,' he began. 'I was never actually asked to go to Maine Road that night by anyone at United and simply went along on my own with intentions of watching the game.

'I travelled across Manchester on the bus after work on the ground staff at Old Trafford, and by some strange piece of good fortune I was seen going through the turnstiles into the ground by a United official. So, when Ray Wood was injured the United staff looked for me, found me and told me to get changed, and the rest is history. I actually had to borrow Colin Webster's boots to play in, as obviously I had nothing there.'

It was certainly a tremendous experience for someone so young to step from the anonymity of junior football to a local derby with a trophy at stake, so how did the debutant adjust to this and his instant fame?

'Surprisingly enough, if it hadn't been for the newspaper coverage the following day, it might all have passed me by,' replied David. 'When I got back to my digs, later than expected, no one would believe that I had played due to the fact that the commentator on the television had been under the impression that Ray Wood had actually returned to the field and resumed playing. Perhaps I should have taken that as a complement! However, when I produced my plaque for playing in the game everyone finally believed that I had actually replaced Ray Wood in goal.'

Despite his inexperience, David, who had not even played at Central League level, certainly did not let himself or the team down and could certainly have claimed to have played a major part in United winning the trophy with a superb last-minute save from Dyson. It was a save that brought instant applause from the players of both sides.

The following day it was back to the normal ground-staff chores for David Gaskell, and it wasn't until 30 November 1958 that he made his second first-team appearance against Tottenham Hotspur at Old Trafford, a game that was not only his League debut but the first First Division fixture that he had actually seen. He made a further two appearances during that season but never really managed to hold down a regular place in the side due to injuries, although he did play in the 1963 FA Cup-winning side.

The prediction of Ian Wooldridge that United were heading back to some form of normality was totally unfounded as United earned the right to compete in the Charity Shield the following season with a second successive League Championship and only missed out on the double with a controversial defeat in the FA Cup Final against Aston Villa.

City did mange to cling on to their First Division status, but it would be some time before they contested the Charity Shield again.

Manchester City: Savage, Leivers, Little, Revie, Ewing, Paul, Fagan, Hayes, Johnstone, Dyson, Clarke.

Manchester United: Wood (substitute Gaskell), Foulkes, Byrne, Colman, Jones, Edwards, Berry, Whelan, Taylor, Viollet, Pegg.

Scorer: Viollet.

Attendance: 30,495.

No. 15

HARTLEPOOLS UNITED V UNITED

5 January 1957

In the first half of the 1956–57 season United had taken Europe by storm, putting 10 past Belgian champions Anderlecht without reply before squeezing past Borussia Dortmund of Germany 3–2 on aggregate. Form in the First Division was equally emphatic, with Matt Busby's team already having the look of champions with the Christmas cards still on the mantelpiece.

The newspaper correspondents of the day were enthusiastic in their praise. 'The greatest soccer machine in the country is what I call them,' wrote Joe Hulme in the *People* after a compelling 3–1 victory over Portsmouth on 29 December, while the 3–1 defeat of Luton at the beginning of that same month saw Peter Slingsby of the *Manchester Evening Chronicle* pen, 'This superbly fit, well-drilled Manchester United outfit is still at the top of the soccer tree and remains the finest advertisement for English football.'

United were not a team of unbeatable supermen, and they seemed to find the FA Cup in particular something of a stumbling block, as a look through the records and previous pages of this book will show. When the draw for the third round of the 1956–57 competition was made, with the name of Manchester United following that of Hartlepools United out of the velvet bag at the Football Association headquarters, there was no sigh of relief that one of their First Division rivals had been avoided, nor any thoughts of an easy passage into round four. Players, club officials and supporters alike were well aware of the embarrassing possibility of an FA Cup giant-killing.

Hartlepools United were long-established members of the Football League Third Division North and were at this particular time enjoying what was arguably the most successful period in the club's history. They were sitting proudly joint top of the Third Division, with 36 points from their 27 games and only goal average separating them from Derby County and Bradford City, the two teams ahead of them.

F.A. CUP — THIRD ROUND
VICTORIA GROUND, WEST HARTLEPOOL

HARTLEPOOLS U.
versus
MANCHESTER U.

SATURDAY, 5th JANUARY, 1957   Kick-off 2-15

ADMIT TO EAST STAND   Reserved Seats

Block C

Nº   476

Row No. .... 2 ....

Seat No. ...... 4 ....

PRICE 8/- (Inc. Tax)

Entrance Marked
CLARENCE ROAD   E

HARTLEPOOLS UNITED

F. C.

OFFICIAL PROGRAMME

SATURDAY, 5th JANUARY, 1957.   **ONE PENNY**

Directors:

President   -   -   -   Mr. W. J. Yeats, J.P.

Mr. H. J. Sargeant, J.P. (*Chairman*)   Mr. W. N. Hope (*Vice-Chairman*)

Mr. H. Atkinson   Mr. H. E. Bailey   Mr. W. Graham   Mr. E. Ord

Mr. T. V. Oldfield   Mr. T. W. Pinkney, J.P.   Mr. S. Spaldin

Mr. W. Usher

Manager: Fred Westgarth, Victoria Ground (Phone 2584)

Secretary: Frank S. Perryman, National Provincial Bank Chambers,
Church Street (Phone 2109)

ORD & PRINTING LIMITED Tower Works Tower Street West Hartlepool.

The 1957 Manchester United team.

In the FA Cup, due to their somewhat lowly status, Hartlepools had to enter the competition from round one, where they were drawn against Selby Town at home. A comfortable 3–1 victory brought an away second-round tie against Blyth Spartans, where a narrow 1–0 win earned them the home draw that every small club secretly longed for.

It was not just the football club that eagerly looked forward to the visit of the current First Division champions. The draw had taken the town by storm, and on the morning of the game fans began queuing outside the ground as early as nine o'clock. By the time the turnstiles opened at one o'clock there was also a sizeable contingent from Manchester in town.

If Hartlepools could not match their illustrious visitors for skill then they could certainly match them for actual playing experience, with several of their players having enjoyed long careers with the north-east club, but at the end of the day it was how each individual performed on that particular afternoon. Little did the record crowd of 17,264 squeezed into the compact ground, having payed £3,470, know what lay in store.

It is worth noting that the record receipts were achieved due to Hartlepools charging double their usual admission prices, with tickets costing four shillings (20p) for adults and two shillings for juniors to stand. Seating in the Clarence Road stand was priced at eight shillings. Despite the once-in-a-lifetime opportunity to see the best team in the country, the local support were far from happy at the club cashing in on United's visit. Perhaps the extension of opening times for the local pubs and working men's clubs acted as a form of compensation to some.

With rain falling and conditions muddy underfoot, the home side won the toss and elected to kick towards the Rink End of the ground, which boasted one of the biggest playing areas in the Northern Division, but those on the packed terracing behind that goal were not about to witness too much in the way of close-up action as United were soon laying siege on the Hartlepool End.

Rather surprisingly it was the United captain, Roger Byrne, who was responsible for the first real threat on the home goal, sending in a teasing, curling shot from 35 yards. Guthrie, however, was well positioned and collected the ball comfortably. Tommy Taylor also featured prominently in those early United attacks, with the 'Pools goalkeeper having to throw himself at the burly United centre's feet as he moved in on goal.

On the counter-attack Frank Stamper headed over the bar, and shortly afterwards the Hartlepools inside-left forced Wood into action. But with only seven minutes gone the inevitable happened. A weak clearance from the Hartlepools defence went only as far as Colman, and the diminutive half-back picked out Liam Whelan, who ran forward to beat the advancing Guthrie with a 20-yard drive. The 'keeper dived too late to keep the ball out.

Before the home side could recover from this undoubted setback they found themselves two down. David Pegg's centre was cleared by the Hartlepools defence, but it fell to the feet of Berry on the right wing, and instead of passing the ball he tried a long-range, angled effort that skimmed across the ground and flew past Guthrie into the back of the net.

2–0 down with a mere eight minutes played was not the news the Hartlepools manager, Fred Westgarth, wanted relayed to his hospital bed, and most of those within the ground thought the visitors were going to run their lesser opponents ragged as they began to threaten with almost every move.

Hartlepools did, however, have their moments, with centre-forward Ken Johnson keeping Mark Jones on his toes. Their best opportunity to pull a goal back fell to Robinson, who, with the goal at his mercy following a Johnson cross, missed the ball completely. A shot from Newton was then headed away by the United centre-half.

With half an hour gone Hartlepools' faint hopes of rescuing something from the game took a decisive blow when Johnson went down with a leg injury and was forced to leave the field for attention. In his absence United attacked the home goal with a vengeance, Whelan and Edwards both coming close, the former having his powerful drive headed out by Moore to the defender's obvious discomfort.

Johnson had barely returned to the fray, clearly struggling, when United went further in front. Tommy Taylor found Whelan unmarked, and the Irishman quickly moved the ball out to Berry, who sent the perfect cross into the Hartlepools goalmouth. The England centre-forward made no mistake, hammering the ball into the roof of the net from close range.

Momentarily silenced, the home crowd were still able to cling to brief glimmers of hope. Five minutes after United's third, Roger Byrne uncharacteristically failed to clear in front of goal, presenting Robinson with something of an easy scoring opportunity, but for the second time in the opening 45 minutes the Hartlepools outside-right failed to grasp the opportunity. Fortunately his error was instantly forgotten as teammate Frank Stamper followed up to drive the ball past Ray Wood to pull a goal back.

The ground erupted in a wall of noise and it was still buzzing as the half-time whistle blew, with United having given the Hartlepools goal another nervous moment following a swift-passing play between Taylor and Pegg that resulted in Berry forcing Guthrie into making yet another fine save. 'Chasing shadows' was how Hartlepools outside-left George Luke described those opening 45 minutes.

Johnny Berry.

Johnson, having left the field limping prior to the interval, returned for the second half at outside-right but was clearly little more than a passenger, and he could do little but watch as United began where they left off, attacking the Hartlepools goal almost at their leisure.

Any home attacks were brought to an almost immediate halt by the imposing figure of Duncan Edwards, and it seemed only a matter of time before another goal would come United's way. Berry and Colman both came close.

Eight minutes into the second half – eight minutes of constant United pressure – Hartlepools broke away down the left. Anderson won possession and played a perfect pass forward to Luke, who scurried forward. Centring the ball towards the right of the United area, away from the defenders, Johnson, clearly thought of as posing little threat by the United defenders, flung himself through the air to head firmly past Wood. It was a goal that was to go down in local folklore.

The volume of noise reached a level of previously unheard proportions, and both the fans and the Hartlepools players sensed that there was still a possibility of creating something of an upset with just over half an hour still to play.

United, for once in the game, looked ruffled. Byrne began to simply boot the ball up-field at every opportunity instead of trying to create attacks with carefully placed passes. The Hartlepools players, on the other hand, suddenly found a new lease of life as the ground buzzed around them, and they began to grow with a confidence that had been missing in the earlier part of the game.

With 25 minutes to go, the impossible happened. Hartlepools' right-half, Jackie Newton, fired the ball into a crowded United goalmouth, and to everyone's amazement the ball flashed past an unsighted Ray Wood and into the corner of the net. Several United defenders had the opportunity to clear the danger prior to Newton's strike, but they were punished for their inability to do so.

Pandemonium ensued, and fortunately neither the press photographer nor the handful of other brave souls who risked life and limb to sit on the roof of the Mill House stand disappeared from view amid the excitement.

Where previously there was hope, there was now belief that the unbelievable could happen and that Hartlepools could indeed overcome their First Division visitors and win the game. It was skill and class up against honest endeavour, post-war austerity against youthful freedom and success.

Many of the home players were experienced journeymen who were nearing the end of their careers and whose fitness levels were considerably lower that their United opponents, and, as the game moved towards the final quarter of an hour, tiredness was beginning to becoming increasingly visible among the home ranks. They were spurned on, however, by the voracious home crowd, who released a deafening roar every time a home player touched the ball.

Guthrie sprang across his goal to deny Taylor, while both Moore and Thompson brought United attacks to a halt, but with 10 minutes remaining the dream was brought to an abrupt end. Berry attempted a shot, which flew across the muddy surface and could only be parried by the Hartlepools goalkeeper. Whelan was the quickest to react and, in a flash, the ball was resting in the back of the net.

It was a killer blow, but despite the hoarse vocal encouragement of the crowd there was nothing left for the home side to give, although Johnson did manage to hit the side netting following a rare attack. The 'ten minute flag', a strange and unusual landmark beside the stand, which was slowly lowered in the final stages of Hartlepools' home games, gradually descended.

At the final whistle both sets of players were quick to congratulate each other, with those in red breathing a sigh of relief at coming through the 90 minutes with a victory.

The United manager, in his 'Matt Busby Talking' column in the *United Review*, wrote in the first home programme after the Cup tie:

> 'What a fight, and what a fright! At Hartlepools, in the Cup tie, you would have said it was all over when United were three goals in the lead after 35 minutes play. But we reckoned without a wonderful fight-back by the Third Division club. It was a splendid game, however, played on a very heavy ground and with rain falling for most of the time.
>
> 'I would like to pay tribute not only to the Hartlepools team for their gallant and brilliant challenge, but to the home spectators who, as you may imagine, never deviated from the course of true sportsmanship, and, at the end, quite freely admitted that United had been the better team. That was echoed in the boardroom, and when I spoke to Mr Fred Westgarth, the Hartlepools manager, who was ill in bed, I assured him that he had every reason to be delighted with the play of his team and that United were certainly worried by the trend of events after the interval. Well played, Hartlepools! We shall never forget your grand struggle and very clean play. You deserved a replay!'

It was a relieved United team that returned south that Saturday evening, but those eventful 90 minutes acted as something of a kick in the pants as the Reds were to score some 27 goals in the next six games – 6–1 at home to Newcastle United, a 2–1 defeat at Sheffield Wednesday, a 5–0 FA Cup win at Wrexham, 4–2 at City, 6–2 against Arsenal at Old Trafford and a 5–1 victory over Charlton at The Valley.

United were on song, and the possibility of a League and Cup double was soon the talk of the terracing, pubs and places of work. But could it be achieved?

Hartlepools United: Guthrie, Cameron, Thompson, Newton, Moore, Anderson, Robinson, McGuigan, Johnson, Stamper, Luke.
Scorer: Stamper, Johnson, Newton.
Manchester United: Wood, Foulkes, Byrne, Colman, Jones, Edwards, Berry, Whelan, Taylor, Viollet, Pegg.
Scorers: Whelan 2, Taylor, Berry.
Attendance: 17,264.

No. 16
UNITED V ATHLETIC BILBAO
6 February 1957

If the Manchester football-loving public had been ecstatic following the 10–0 hammering of Anderlecht in that European Cup preliminary-round second-leg tie at Maine Road, thinking that they would never witness a better, more enthralling and captivating 90 minutes, then they were soon to be proved wrong.

Borussia Dortmund, the German champions had been narrowly defeated 3–2 in front of a crowd of 75,598 in the first round first leg, a much more respectable attendance compared with that of the Anderlecht game and the highest recorded at Maine Road since 1934. But the overall performance on the night was far from convincing, with Frank Taylor of the *News Chronicle* going as far as calling the United players 'cocky', while pointing the finger at Roger Byrne 'for a slip that started an avalanche of Borussia attacks,' at Eddie Colman and Duncan Edwards 'for not getting a grip of the game,' and at Tommy Taylor and Liam Whelan 'for not bringing their wingers into the game more'. Taylor even suggested that 'a single-goal lead is not likely to be enough when the second leg is played in Dortmund'.

United more or less began the match as they had left off against Anderlecht, taking the lead in the 11th minute through Dennis Viollet, with the same player making it 2–0 a quarter of an hour later. Ten minutes prior to the interval a David Pegg shot was deflected past the Borussia goalkeeper by Burgsmueller for a third. Kwiatkowski, in a green jersey borrowed from fellow countryman and City goalkeeper Bert Trautmann, had to make several outstanding saves to keep the scoreline down. The crowd, although perhaps not expecting to see United hit double figures for a second consecutive European fixture, did anticipate further goals in the second 45 minutes.

The crowd certainly got more goals, but they were not for United as the gold-shirted Germans slowly took control of the game, scoring twice and leaving United clinging on to their slender advantage.

In the second leg, on a pitch more akin to a skating rink, United managed by the skin of their teeth to keep the Germans at bay, with Frank Taylor on this occasion praising Roger Byrne and his fellow defender, Mark Jones, along with goalkeeper Ray Wood for their part in seeing United through to the quarter-finals.

Lying in wait were Athletic Bilbao, with the first leg in Spain on 16 January. It was not sunny Spain, however, as snow fell throughout the game and the pitch, where it was not covered in snow, was a patch of mud. Despite those atrocious conditions, which Bilbao mastered superbly, their play showed why they had only been beaten once at home in the past three years.

ATLETICO DE BILBAO v. MANCHESTER UNITED, 16th JANUARY, 1957

Photo by Associated Press

At half-time United were 3–0 down, but to their credit they did manage to pull it back to 3–2 through Taylor and Viollet. However, they were soon to find themselves once again three goals behind as the Spaniards fought back to score twice and put United's future in the European Cup very much in the balance. The odds improved slightly five minutes from time, when Liam Whelan scored a third for United, giving them a glimmer of hope back in Manchester.

The Spaniards flew into Manchester full of confidence, with captain Augustin Gainza making a 0–0 sign with his fingers as he happily posed for photographs. Perhaps there was also a hint of hope in his prediction, as he, along with his teammates, was on £200 per man to progress into the semi-finals. Bilbao had put so much emphasis on this particular fixture that they had played nine reserves in a League game against Barcelona the previous Sunday, a game that they had lost 2–0. United, on the other hand, fielded a full-strength side against City in the 4–2 win at Maine Road, but any inclination by Matt Busby to do otherwise would have resulted in a hefty fine from the Football League.

Despite the possibility of seeing United going out of the competition, supporters eagerly snatched up the tickets as soon as they went on sale, though many were left disappointed because the Maine Road capacity was cut to 65,000, some 10,000 fewer than had clicked through the turnstiles for the Dortmund tie. One supporter, desperate to see the games, gladly paid a tout £11 for stand ticket. Others, who had bought forged tickets, were not so fortunate and were turned away at the turnstiles.

But 65,000 can still make a formidable noise, and the crowd was certainly vocal in their encouragement of Matt Busby's team as they took to the Maine Road pitch in an effort to overturn the Spaniards' two-goal lead. Patience, however, was the name of the game as the Spaniards were certainly in no hurry, simply content to play for time from the outset, but United were somewhat over-anxious, spending little time on the ball and shooting quicker than any gunslinger from the Wild West.

The crowd were momentarily silenced early on when Mark Jones slipped while making a tackle, but any danger was soon averted and a sigh of relief echoed around the ground when the United centre-half, who had fallen awkwardly, got up and rejoined the fray.

Try as United might, the Spaniards repelled everything that came their way, leaving United and their supporters frustrated as the first half wore on. Had United used their wing men more then perhaps things might have been different, but with play more often than not down the middle, the highly organised Spanish defence coped without much of a problem. That was, however, until four minutes before the interval.

From the touchline Matt Busby urged Duncan Edwards to push further forward in support of the attack, and as the ball arrived at the feet of the United left-half, Edwards unleashed a powerful drive in the direction of the Bilbao goal. On target and with the power to beat the goalkeeper, Carmelo, more in hope than anything else, right-half Mauri stuck his foot out and momentarily slowed the flight of the ball towards goal but diverted it towards the lurking Viollet, who wasted little time in shooting past the Bilbao 'keeper.

The roar that greeted that goal was twice surpassed within three minutes of the second half getting under way, but on both occasions it was followed by groans of disbelief and boos of

95

Liam Whelan.

disagreement as both goals were disallowed by the referee for offside. The raised linesman's flag denied Viollet and then Whelan, the German referee later saying that the second, more controversial, of the two, was disallowed because Whelan had been in an offside position when he nudged Viollet's goal-bound header over the line.

Although disappointed by both decisions, protesting profusely at the second and momentarily losing their grip on the game, all United could do was keep plodding away in the hope that they would finally get the break that their play deserved. Pegg shot wide from only six yards out and Taylor hit the post, but still the goal that could change the game would not come.

With less than 20 minutes remaining, United were still clinging on to those slender hopes as Tommy Taylor collected an Eddie Colman free-kick, brushed past Garay and fired a left-footed shot that beat Carmelo and went in off the post.

United now had the bit between their teeth and, with the cheering still vibrating around the ground, they scored a third with only six minutes remaining, and it was Tommy Taylor who was once again the thorn in the Bilbao side. Gathering the ball on the right, the England player managed to avoid the attention of Garay and moved towards the byline. Glancing up, he noticed the diminutive figure of Johnny Berry, the pair having switched places, moving forward

Tommy Taylor scores United's second against Bilbao.

through the middle and, cutting the ball back, the on-running 31-year-old United winger side-footed the ball home.

Realising the game was now slipping away from them, Bilbao, with nothing to lose, pushed forward and, with the seconds ticking away, almost forced a play-off in Paris. A mis-kick presented Gainza with an opportunity, but Ray Wood slid across his muddy goalmouth to save. Another Spanish attack forced a corner, but the referee's whistle ended any hopes of that dramatic recovery.

Ecstatic crowds gathered around the players' entrance outside the ground, offering their congratulations as their heroes left for the after-match dinner at the Midland Hotel, a meal of hare soup, sole fried in butter, roast lamb, fruit salad and cheeses.

The following morning's newspapers replayed the game for those elated supporters, and for once there was no doubt that the frequently read reporters had been at the same game as the fans, with the pressmen equally as enthusiastic in their thoughts of the game and their praise for the United players. 'That magic moment, five minutes from time, when Maine Road went mad and United were – All Berry And Bright!' proclaimed the *Daily Mirror* above Archie Ledbrooke's report. 'Call this the match of the century? Don't know, I haven't lived that long. But I do know that this was one of the matches I'll never forget, one of the best half-dozen I've seen in nearly 2,000. The crowd of 65,000 will say this morning that they've never seen anything like it. They are probably right.'

In the *News Chronicle*, Frank Taylor wrote, 'Hail the Busby Braves! For 90 thrill-packed minutes under the Maine Road floodlights last night the champions of England pounded the Spanish champions until they were sunk by a three-goal salvo. What a triumph for Matt Busby! What a triumph for British football.' He went on, 'It was the most nerve-wracking game I have ever sat through. I thrilled as United pulled back one goal, then two, then shot into the lead and into the last four of the European Cup. At the finish 65,000 fans sang and cheered the triumph of these young soccer stars from Old Trafford. But when I saw the team in the dressing room they could hardly raise a smile. They had run themselves into the ground. They were too tired to even sing.'

The *Daily Express* and Henry Rose were little different. 'Manchester Magnifico,' read the headline, with 'Greatest Victory in Soccer History' underneath. 'My hands are still trembling,' wrote Rose. 'My heart still pounds. And a few hours have passed since, with 65,000 lucky people, I saw the greatest soccer victory in history, 90 minutes of tremendous thrill and excitement that will live for ever in the memory. Salute the 11 red-shirted heroes of Manchester United, the whole country is proud of you. Hammering in my brain, almost shattering my senses, is the still-fresh memory of 11 brave, gallant footballers battering, pounding until they had them on their knees almost crying for mercy, a team of Spaniards ranked as one of the best club teams in the world.'

They couldn't all be wrong!

Sadly, a year to the day, Rose and Ledbrooke would die on a slush-covered Munich runway alongside most of those players of whom they sung the praises for defeating Bilbao. Taylor was severely injured but lived to recall his memories of those excellent days in 'The Team That Wouldn't Die'.

United were in the semi-final, where they were unfortunate to be paired with another Spanish side, the mighty Real Madrid, the holders of the European Cup. It would be a stern test for Busby's team but one that would allow him to judge just how far his team had come and how good they actually were.

Today, much is made of mid-week games taking too much out of the players, but back in the 1950s, when the playing attire and balls were heavier and pitches were in a much poorer condition, they simply got on with it without complaint.

Three days after being drenched with sweat in the defeat of Bilbao, Busby fielded the same 11 players for the visit from Arsenal to Old Trafford and, with little sign of tiredness or whatever it is that the modern day players and managers often complain about, United ran their visitors ragged, winning 6–2.

Manchester United: Wood, Foulkes, Byrne, Colman, Jones, Edwards, Berry, Whelan, Taylor, Viollet, Pegg.
Scorers: Viollet, Taylor, Berry.
Athletic Bilbao: Carmelo, Orue, Canito, Mauri, Garay, Maguregui, Arteche, Maracaida, Eture, Merodio, Gainza.
Attendance: 65,000.

No. 17

UNITED V BOLTON WANDERERS
25 March 1957

The first attempts at floodlit football came in the early winter evenings of 1878. On 14 October at Bramall Lane, Sheffield United erected lamps on wooden gantries for a match between the Reds and the Blues, two teams made up of players from the local sides, while a month later Blackburn Rovers carried out a similar experiment with Accrington in opposition. But it wasn't until the immediate post-war years that thoughts turned to floodlit football on a more regular basis, with Wolverhampton Wanderers being pioneers in this venture, playing host to a South African XI, Racing Club of Argentina and the more familiar continental names of Spartak Moscow and Honved in 1953.

United were also quick to bring a touch of foreign football to the North West, with games against the likes of Red Star Belgrade and Hapoel, but those games were played in daylight and failed to conjure up the same magic as the fixtures played out at Molineux.

Even Manchester City were one step ahead of their more illustrious neighbours when it came to installing floodlights, with the United directors having to hire Maine Road for the early sojourns into European football, but it wasn't as if United had not looked into the matter; under Matt Busby they were not a club to stand still or be left behind.

In the *United Review* for the match against Portsmouth on 1 September 1956 the club unveiled their own plans for floodlights at Old Trafford, with an illustration on the front page of a model of the stadium complete with the pylons. The accompanying text read as follows: 'According to electrical experts we should have a floodlighting system as good, if not better, than any installation in the country! From the model photographed here you will see four pylons, each to be 160 feet high. At the top of each tower will be 54 floodlights – equal to millions of candle power – and the whole installation will be controlled by a single button. The work has been commissioned and completion is expected early in the New Year.' The expected cost was to be over £40,000.

The erection of the floodlights at Old Trafford had gone according to plan, and they were due to be used for the first time when Lancashire neighbours Bolton Wanderers visited on 23 March. This gave Bolton the distinction of being the first visitors after the war and also the first to play under the new lights, three of which were unusually situated outside the ground.

Approaching the ground on the night, the sky around Old Trafford was aglow in the evening air as the spectators, attracted like moths, almost ran towards the ground, determined to enjoy as much as possible of this unique occasion.

A Sunday Express Picture

Not for the first time the 'House Full' notices appeared, the gates locked about half an hour before kick-off with many still outside and traffic having already come to a standstill on Chester Road some 30 minutes previously. Seventy extra police officers had to be called to the ground to deal with the estimated 15,000 who were stranded outside, with 60,862 shoulder-to-shoulder inside.

While the press handout said that the lights would produce the effect of continuous sunlight, the 90-minutes that followed produced nothing but gloom for the United players and supporters alike, and those who had hurried towards the turnstiles were soon to wish that they had walked at their normal pace towards the ground and had found themselves locked out.

Bolton Wanderers arrived at Old Trafford having already beaten the reigning champions 2–0 a few miles up the road at Burnden Park, but they were among the also-rans in the First Division title chase, languishing in eighth position, some 13 points behind United.

They could also be considered something of a bogey team for United, as home and away victories had not been claimed against them since season 1949–50. Indeed, United had only won two League fixtures against their near neighbours in the past four seasons and had suffered a humiliating 5–1 home defeat against them in 1953–54.

As the supporters who had managed to gain admission prior to the gates being shut stood marvelling at the lights, like young children at a fairground, United added some colour to the occasion by running from the tunnel and onto the field in their new, all-red strip, an outfit that they would also wear against Real Madrid in the two European Cup fixtures the following month. But it was Bolton who were to dazzle under the lights, and not simply because of their all-white, Real Madrid look-a-like outfit.

The visitors had enjoyed a weekend off from the rigours of First Division football. United had also managed a weekend away from defending their First Division championship but were involved in an FA Cup semi-final tie against Birmingham City at Sheffield Wednesday's Hillsborough ground. Despite not playing to their capabilities, they still managed to overcome their opponents, who were also well below par, winning 2–0 and reaching the Final for the first time since 1948, keeping their hopes of a domestic double on line.

Forty-eight hours later it was back to League business, searching for another two points to keep the title hopes alive, but as the evening unfolded some dark shadows were cast amid the glare from the towering pylons around the ground as the visitors recorded a 2–0 victory.

United looked tired as Bolton made a lively start, and twice the home crowd winced as Gubbins shot narrowly past and it looked a certainty that he would score. His fellow teammates harassed and harried United, forcing them into errors and preventing them from settling or creating chances of their own.

Berry did manage to get the home crowd buzzing with a winding run, which ended with something of an opportunistic shot amid a packed goalmouth, but this was a rare opportunity and the crowd were soon returned to their rather subdued mood.

Despite their superiority, it took the visitors half an hour to take the lead. A cross-field pass from Lofthouse caught the United defence flat, and Gubbins ran onto the ball before passing to the better-positioned Parry, who beat Wood to score.

Bill Foulkes.

The goal seemed to give United something of a wake-up call, with Pegg, Berry and makeshift centre-forward Duncan Edwards all going close. Edwards, despite his undoubted versatility, looked a little out of place playing so far forward and only managed one real shot on target. But despite their rather infrequent efforts, the Bolton defence stood firm and United failed to show their real attacking flair.

Four minutes into the second half United conceded a second goal, much to the disappointment of players and crowd alike. With the linesman flagging for a foul against Wilf McGuinness, Hartle, whether actually meaning to or whether simply just booting it in frustration, kicked the ball towards the United goal from around 40 yards out, where it struck Foulkes on the side of the head and flew past Wood for an own-goal. The crowd was certainly not impressed and booed as the United players protested, but the goal stood.

If the first goal came as a wake-up call, the second really stirred the home side into action and they surged forward in search of both revenge and a goal in order to keep the game alive, with shots raining down on the Bolton goal from all angles.

Busby, sensing that he had to do something, appeared on the touchline and shouted to Duncan Edwards and Jackie Blanchflower to change places, but it was to little avail as Bolton, content with their two goals and realising that they were in a strong position to take both points, simply fell back and defended. Even Nat Lofthouse could be found near the Bolton goal when United had a corner-kick.

As much as they tried, United just could not break down the numerous white shirts in front of them and were made to look rather indifferent in front of their own supporters. Hopkinson was called into action, saving brilliantly from both Berry and Edwards. He stopped one effort from the latter with his foot and watched rather helplessly as the ball spun high in the air. Pegg hit the ball into the side netting, while Charlton had an effort blocked, but all credit must be given to the visitors, who came to Old Trafford with a definitive game plan and adhered to it throughout the 90 minutes. According to Archie Ledbrooke in the *Daily Mirror*, 'They didn't just beat the treble-chasing champions, THEY THRASHED THEM.'

In the *Daily Express*, Henry Rose wrote, 'History, they say, is made at night. Bolton Wanderers certainly made soccer history last night when they became the first club this season to complete the double over Manchester United, Great Britain's show team.'

What did the spectators think of Old Trafford's latest additions? Among the crowd that night was schoolboy Tom Clare, who recalled the following: 'I would normally have travelled to Old Trafford by bus and be at the ground very early to secure myself a place down at the front of the Popular Side and up against the picket fence, which surrounded the shale perimeter around the playing pitch.

'On this occasion though, things turned out to be a little different. Our local chip shop, which was on the corner of our street, was owned by a man named Alf Taylor. Although a United fan, he didn't actually attend many United matches, but this time, along with his son, Fred, he decided to go and to see the "switching on" of the lights. Knowing how enthusiastic I was about Manchester United, Mr Taylor invited me to travel with them in his car to the match. It was too good an opportunity for a young 12-year-old to refuse, and I thought what a tale I would have to tell the kids at school the following morning – me, travelling to the match by car!

'What should have been such an enjoyable experience actually turned into something that was almost a nightmare. We set out from Rusholme Road, in Chorlton upon Medlock, around 5:45pm. What should have been nothing more than a 20-minute journey was baulked by heavy traffic, and, as we got close to Old Trafford itself, the lack of a parking space. Mr. Taylor eventually found a spot on Elsinore Road at the back of Old Trafford Station after circumnavigating the area. I was away like lightning as I wanted to be inside that stadium as quickly as possible. Before I left, Mr Taylor said we would all meet back at the car once the match was over, and off I ran.

'I came under the railway underpass and out besides Lancashire CCC on Warwick Road, and you could tell even then that there was going to be a larger than normal attendance. My little legs ran as fast as they could, and as the evening had started to darken I could see the floodlights atop of the pylons shining like beacons. Over Talbot Road and then down across Chester Road I ran, and more and more people seemed to be making their way down to the ground past the United Café and the railway bridge and onto what then passed as the forecourt of the ground. Huge queues of people lined up from the turnstile entrances, and I managed to make my way around onto United Road and where the Juniors' turnstile was on the Popular Side. Again I passed huge queues at the other turnstiles, and by the time that I had gained entrance into the stadium it was well past 7pm.

'Trying to make my way down the terracing towards my favourite vantage point proved very difficult, and I came to an abrupt halt. As I jumped and tried to see if there was a way down, a complete stranger saw my situation and got hold of me and hoisted me onto the concrete foundation of one of the crash barriers. What a breath-taking view – the Old Trafford pitch in all its glory under the new floodlights. Because of where I was standing I could not actually see the floodlights, but the magnificence was there for all to see and, as the light faded, the scene was a joy to behold.

'Outside of the stadium there was mayhem as apparently, shortly after I had gained entrance, all the turnstiles were closed and thousands of fans were locked out. Over 60,000 fans were inside, some 15,000 more than the normal average attendance. Many had travelled from Bolton and the Trotters had more than a good number in support. The atmosphere was certainly heightened by the occasions, and both teams came onto the field to massive receptions from their fans.

'As the darkness fell it was so easy to see everything clearly – United in all red, and Bolton in all white, the lines on the pitch easily visible, and they were playing with a white ball. There was often a misconception about the white match ball back in those days. Some pundits used to say that it was much lighter than the regular match ball, but that was nothing more than a myth. The pitch markings were probably so easy to see under the lights because at that time of the season, the pitch was definitely only on nodding terms with the thing called grass!

105

'The white ball didn't do United too many favours that evening as the game was lost 2–0, and Bolton once again had walked away with the two points. Whether the occasion got to United's young side it was hard to tell. Certainly there was plenty of vocal encouragement for them, especially from that Popular Side. The formation of the team was also changed a little due to the fact that Duncan Edwards played at centre-forward in place of Tommy Taylor, who was out injured, and Dennis Viollet had aggravated his groin further when playing in the FA Cup semi-final the previous Saturday, so the young Wilf McGuinness came in at left-half and Duncan moved up front.

'The one thing that I will always remember from the match itself was a wonderful headed goal. The scorer flew through air like a bird, connecting with the ball full on, and it rocketed into the back of the net, leaving the goalkeeper absolutely stranded. Unfortunately for United the scorer was Bill Foulkes, and the goal was an own-goal. Bolton added a second goal later on and the match was over as a contest from that point onwards. The final whistle went and the crowds started to leave the stadium. I can recall it was very difficult getting across the forecourt and even more difficult with crowding upon the railway bridge and then all the way up to Chester Road. Once across, I ran all the way back to Elsinore Road.

'When I got there I was in a panic. There was no car where I had left it and no sign of Mr Taylor and his son. I waited and waited, and then it dawned on me that they must not have been able to get in and had returned back home. Obviously they had no way of letting me know. I walked back home and it was almost past 11pm when I arrived. Mum was absolutely frantic, and when I explained to her what had happened she was none too pleased with Mr Taylor.

'The floodlights were a huge hit with the United fans and became a very prominent feature on Manchester's skyline from many vantage points throughout the City. Over the next 30 years or so, many truly magnificent matches were witnessed under their glare by hundreds of thousands of fans who travelled not only from all parts of Britain and Europe but also many parts of the world.'

Manchester United: Wood, Foulkes, Byrne, Colman, Blanchflower, McGuinness, Berry, Whelan, Edwards, Charlton, Pegg.
Bolton Wanderers: Hopkinson, Hartle, Ball, Hennin, Edwards, Bell, Holden, Stevens, Lofthouse, Parry, Gubbins.
Scorers: Parry, Foulkes (own-goal).
Attendance: 60,862.

No. 18

UNITED V REAL MADRID

25 April 1957

Having shown Europe that they were more than capable of holding their own with the emphatic victories over Anderlecht and Bilbao, a semi-final pairing with Fiorentina would have been much more acceptable to Manchester United than being drawn against the might of Real Madrid.

The Italians had only reached the last four due to a solitary-goal victory against Red Star Belgrade, scored in the 88th minute of the first leg in the Yugoslavian capital, and they would certainly not have caused United too many problems over the two legs. It would also have been more favourable to have met the Spaniards in a one-off game at a neutral venue than face them in the first leg at their fortified bastion of the Bernabéu.

Results in the run-up to the crunch match in Spain were certainly far from favourable. After having blasted their way through February with a 4–2 victory over Manchester City, 6–2 against Arsenal, a 1–0 FA Cup victory over Everton and the 5–1 thumping of Charlton Athletic, the last fixture of that month produced something of a shock when Blackpool extracted some form of revenge for the previous season with a 2–0 win at Old Trafford.

March, as far as League results went, was disappointing, with only six points from five games. Victories came against Everton and Leeds United, points were shared against Aston Villa and Wolverhampton Wanderers, and sweet nothing was gained from Bolton's visit to Old Trafford. The latter was even more disappointing as it marked the first fixture under the new floodlights, but there was certainly no dazzling display from the home side as they struggled through the match, often wishing that someone would actually pull the plug and the ground would plunge into darkness.

A 0–0 draw at home to Tottenham Hotspur the weekend prior to the first leg of the semi-final was not the ideal confidence booster, but on the plus side there were no injury problems for Matt Busby's team as the United party flew out to Madrid.

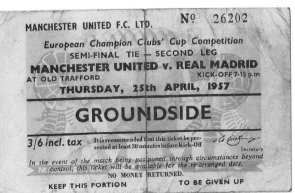

MANCHESTER UNITED WELCOME REAL MADRID

Esta noche, el Manchester United Football Club se unirá a los aficionados al fútbol de todo el Reino Unido para ofrecer al Real Madrid la más cordial y sincera bienvenida deportiva.

Esta noche, dos de los equipos de fútbol más celebrados en Europa lucharán por el privilegio del encuentro competidor final en el que se adjudicará la copa de plata al vencedor en el European Champion Club Competition.

Aunque el Real Madrid es un formidable oponente con su record deportivo sin igual, nosotros también poseemos titulos honorificos que los Campeones Espanoles hallan dignos de respeto. Pero cualquiera que sea el resultado de este partido memorable, démos las gracias a los perspicaces organizadores de este encuentro, no sólo por haber reunido los más finos exponentes del fútbol, sino también por aumentar la amistad sincera entre los deportistas de Europa.

United were given a warm welcome in the Spanish capital, with 134,000 packing the Bernabéu on the night of the match – the biggest crowd recorded in the competition to date – but below the towering terracing, the Madrid players showed little in the way of hospitality towards their guests.

'Madrid Got Away With Murder', wrote Archie Ledbrooke in the *Daily Mirror*, telling his avid readers that 'the Babes were kicked, tripped, outplayed,' while the game was a 'rough house, with 14 fouls in the first 17 minutes'.

Playing in an all-red strip, United matched their hosts for that opening 45 minutes and could well have scored twice in the first half. Tommy Taylor lost control when about to shoot, and then Johnny Berry was brought down from behind in the penalty area but the referee looked the other way. United matched their hosts for that opening 45 minutes.

With the second half only 15 minutes old, Madrid went a goal in front, Rial diving to head home a Gento cross. A quarter of an hour later it was 2–0. This time Di Stefano ghosted through the United defence before slipping the ball past Wood as he moved off his line.

Despite going two goals behind, United kept pressing forward whenever possible, and their resilience was rewarded eight minutes from time when Tommy Taylor threw himself at a Whelan centre to put his team right back into the game.

It was now the home side who were on the defensive. Whelan saw a shot go narrowly wide while Viollet sent one just over, but with a mere five minutes remaining, disaster struck. Having halted yet another United attack, Madrid broke away down the left, with Mateos, Gento and Rial passing the ball between them before Mateos scored from close in.

It was something of an injustice, but both manager Matt Busby and captain Roger Byrne felt that the tie was far from over. 'Madrid were the better side. It was a big occasion,' said the United manager. 'I still think we have a chance. Our defensive play was splendid.'

Roger Byrne certainly agreed with his manager, saying, 'Madrid are a good team, but the bounce of the ball did not go our way. I think we can win the return, as we did against Bilbao. We should have had a penalty when Berry was brought down.'

Kopa slides the ball into the net.

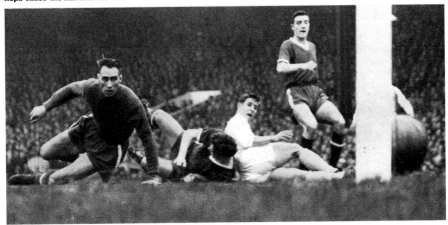

Ledbrooke, on the other hand, was quick to point his finger at the referee. 'He should have sent Di Stefano off the field for kicking Blanchflower. He passed a blatant trip on Berry.' He also reported that Billy Whelan was kicked in the stomach, but again the Dutch official took no action.

At 2–1 United had more than a chance of overcoming the current holders at Old Trafford, but, requiring two goals just to pull level, although not impossible, it was a difficult task indeed.

Prior to Madrid's visit, United, although looking slightly tired, defeated Luton Town 2–0 at Kenilworth Road, beat Burnley 3–1 at Turf Moor thanks to a Liam Whelan hat-trick, and then clinched their second successive League Championship with a resounding 4–0 home win over Sunderland at Old Trafford.

Having ensured that the Championship trophy would remain in Manchester for at least another year, Busby made wholesale changes to the team he sent out against Burnley three days before Real Madrid came to town. He left out Byrne, Jones, Blanchflower, Edwards, Berry, Whelan, Taylor, Charlton and Pegg, bringing in Greaves, Goodwin, Cope, McGuinness, Webster, Doherty, Dawson, Viollet and Scanlon, but it made little difference to the result as United ran out 2–0 winners.

With Old Trafford now having its own floodlighting system there was no cross-Manchester journey to Maine Road needed in order to host the home leg of the European Cup semi-final against the reigning champions. Television rights were secured by Granada, with the whole match scheduled to be shown live, much to the disappointment of the BBC, who had been caught by surprise with their rival's move.

Granada's securing of those television rights, however, did give them a few problems in the run-up to the match. They planned to use three cameras, but finding ideal positions for them proved to be difficult. Each side of the ground had covered accommodation, and placing cameras near the halfway line would mean blocking the view of a few spectators. Using either end of the ground behind the goals would mean that, although they would be above the heads of the crowd, they would perhaps be too far from some of the action. A camera in the main stand would mean the removal of some seats, and as architects, along with stress and strain experts, were called in, it was even suggested that part of the stand roof could be cut away to accommodate the necessary equipment. In the end, ideal positions were found behind the goals and along the side. Everyone was happy, with the exception of the BBC!

Real Madrid arrived in Manchester to defend their two-goal advantage, disappointed that some United supporters, having no doubt read Archie Ledbrooke's match report of the first leg, gave them some abuse when they arrived at their Manchester hotel. It was, however, only a mere warm-up for what they about to endure at Old Trafford.

Upon arriving at the ground the day prior to the game, Real Madrid almost called the fixture off as they discovered that, whether due to gamesmanship or otherwise, Busby had given orders for the Old Trafford pitch to be watered and, with sand having already been added in places, the pitch, as far as Real Madrid were concerned, was far from ideal. They politely but firmly told the United officials that if they did not desist from watering the pitch, something that they had apparently been doing for several days, then they would refuse to play. Rather reluctantly, the sprinklers were turned off, and where the pitch was soft more sand was scattered.

Outside Old Trafford leading up to the kick-off, the police found themselves in the unusual position of giving away hundreds of tickets as supporters with spares found it difficult to get rid of them and, not wanting to hang about outside the ground, gave them to the police. Even the ticket touts had difficulty selling their wares, offering £1 tickets for four shillings (20p).

The game began in a similar fashion to the first leg, with Madrid being penalised for a foul as early as the first 30 seconds and a further four following in as many minutes. Their defenders were somewhat unsettled by the baying crowd, but Di Stefano managed to apply some sort of stability in midfield by keeping a cool head as the noise from the touchline increased.

Despite the *Manchester Evening Chronicle* having distributed several thousand red-and-white paper caps and red-and-white megaphones in order to increase the volume and add to the scene prior to what they termed as the 'greatest-ever match at Old Trafford', the game, with 25 minutes gone and United having only had one shot at goal, was effectively over as a contest as Madrid increased their advantage to 4–1. Di Stefano, as always, got the move under way, passing to Rial, who in turn threaded the ball through to Kopa, who slipped the ball past the advancing Wood. Eight minutes later United were two behind on the night. Gento beat Foulkes comfortably before slipping the ball across the front of the United goal for Rial to score.

Blanchflower's superb defensive play managed to keep the scoreline to 2–0 at the interval, but the men in the forward line in front of him were too casual and certainly did not look like the team that everyone knew they could be.

There must have been words spoken in the home dressing room at the interval because after the break, with the evening breeze behind them, United began to look more effective. Colman moved forward on a more regular basis while Edwards took the game by the scruff of the neck, leading a non-stop attack on the Madrid goal.

One minute over the hour United pulled a goal back. A quick throw-in went from Byrne to Pegg, and the winger, having found space, crossed into the area, where Tommy Taylor forced the ball home in a packed goalmouth at the second attempt.

Was there still the possibility of United clawing something from the game? A back header from Taylor was stopped by Alonso. The Spanish 'keeper then dived full length to stop another effort from the former Barnsley centre sneaking over the line. Another Taylor shot was stopped by Alonso, but he failed to hold it and the ball had to be scrambled away by one of his fellow defenders.

Time was slowly running away from United, and despite Bobby Charlton scoring a second with four minutes to go, hitting home a Pegg cross and levelling the score on the night, everyone present had been aware for some time that there were not going to be any United heroics on the night.

The final 10 minutes of this rather drab and disappointing encounter captured most of the headlines the following morning as there were scenes that no one had expected nor indeed wanted to see.

'Forty-eight fouls and a free-for-all disgrace; a soccer showpiece,' ran across the top of the *Daily Express* above the match report from Henry Rose.'United's effort was born of desperation. It was bereft of the skill, rhythm, class and polish that has charmed the sporting world. I wish

I could end the story with just the names of the goalscorers. I hate having to write more for I am still angered by 90 minutes of vicious, bad-tempered football by two of the world's star teams.

He continued, 'And what a shambling, disgraceful last four minutes. Just after Bob Charlton made it 2–2 in the 84th minute, Manuel Torres, the right-back Madrid imported for the occasion, fell in a heap near the goal and touchline. He was surrounded quickly by angry, gesticulating players in what looked like a free-for-all. The referee wanted Torres to go off; United players rushed to help in the operation. Madrid pulled Torres back.

'I ASK YOU WHAT SORT OF STUFF IS THIS?

'The scenes did not end there. When play restarted, inside-right Mateos was seen to collapse after a collision with Roger Byrne. The Spaniard rose unsteadily then collapsed again. All the time the crowd booed what they considered was a bad piece of play acting.

'And at the final whistle, Matt Busby hurried onto the pitch and protested to the referee that he had whistled up without allowing time for stoppages.'

Liam Whelan was later to add, 'Soon after our second goal I saw the Spanish trainer signalling six minutes to go. Seconds later the final whistle went. I was surprised.'

Many, however, had not seen those final minutes, as the *Daily Herald* reported that 'thousands left the ground well before the end,' while that particular paper's man at the match, George Follows, wrote of 'a squalid show of one-eyed partisanship...a public display of bad manners...they wanted physical revenge.'

In his report, Follows also wrote this of the crowd: 'They bombarded two Spanish men and a girl fan with empty cartons as they carried a Madrid banner round the ground at half-time. They incited Edwards and Byrne into actions that they will want to forget.'

The dreams of beating Real Madrid had turned into a nightmare, and the hopes of lifting three trophies in one season evaporated into the cold Manchester air. It was to be some 42 years before such dreams came true, while revenge against the Spanish giants took a mere 11.

Manchester United: Wood, Foulkes, Byrne, Colman, Blanchflower, Edwards, Berry, Whelan, Taylor, Charlton, Pegg.
Scorers: Taylor, Charlton.
Real Madrid: J. Alonso, Torres, Lesmes, Munos, M. Alonso, Zarrga, Kopa, Mateos, Di Stefano, Rial, Gento
Scorers: Kopa, Rial.
Attendance: 65,000.

No. 19
UNITED V ASTON VILLA
4 May 1957

Wembley Stadium, in days gone by and before money became the root of all evil within the game, was a venue that only the select few were able to boast that they had been privileged to play at, making that long walk up the sloping tunnel and into the vast bowl of noise.

If you were good enough, international recognition would enable you to play there on one of the handful of occasions that saw representative games scattered though the annual fixture lists. If, however, you were a mere mortal whose playing ability fell short of the standards required by the team manager or selection committee (who often had a bigger say in whether or not a player made the international side), then your only hope of making the journey up Wembley Way towards the twin towers was on Cup Final day.

Today Wembley does not hold the same magic of old due to financial greed, with everything from Play-off Finals and FA Cup semi-finals taking place there, removing that special dream that made playing in the FA Cup Final itself so very special.

It is the dream of countless supporters across the country to stand at Wembley Stadium on Cup Final day and sing *Abide With Me*. Like many players, most fans had to wait a number of years to fulfil this ambition, and despite United losing unexpectedly to Southampton, supporters this year could always say that they had been at an FA Cup Final. Thankfully, unlike many players, they were to experience happier days below the twin towers.

United supporters of an older generation had a long wait for the opportunity of a May trip to Wembley to materialise. For those who had marvelled at the skills of Billy Meredith, the strength of Roberts and Duckworth and the goals of Sandy Turnbull and George Wall, there was no Wembley in 1909 but the surrogate venue of Crystal Palace. For a large majority of those who were unable to attend the 1–0 victory over Bristol City, there was not going to be a 'never mind, I will get to the next one,' as it was some 39 years before the name of Manchester United appeared on the FA Cup Final programme again.

Having been made homeless by the bombardment of nearby Trafford Park in World War Two, United

THE FOOTBALL ASSOCIATION CHALLENGE CUP COMPETITION

FINAL TIE
ASTON VILLA
v
MANCHESTER UNITED

SATURDAY, MAY 4th, 1957   KICK-OFF 3 pm

EMPIRE STADIUM

WEMBLEY

OFFICIAL PROGRAMME   -   ONE SHILLING

were forced to take up a temporary tenancy with neighbours City, something that was to cause minor problems in their 1948 Cup campaign.

Drawn at 'home' against Liverpool in round four, they had to relocate to Everton's Goodison Park, and in round five, drawn at 'home' again, this time against Charlton Athletic, it was off to Leeds Road, Huddersfield, both because City had also been drawn at home and obviously had first call on their Maine Road ground.

Away ties took them to Aston Villa and Preston North End and, having progressed to the semi-final, it was over the Pennines to Sheffield Wednesday's Hillsborough to fight for a place in the Final against Blackpool. United overcame the difficulties of playing every game away from home and defeated their Lancashire neighbours 4–2 in one of the best Finals ever seen at Wembley.

It was, however, to be another nine years before Matt Busby led his team out at Wembley again, and few who witnessed the previously mentioned third-round tie against Hartlepools United would have imagined that United could go all the way to the Final. They certainly made up for their rather inept performance in the North East with a crushing 5–0 victory in North Wales against Wrexham, goals coming from Whelan (2), Taylor (2) and Byrne.

Round four brought First Division rivals Everton to Old Trafford and, having already been beaten 5–2 at home back in October by the Goodison Park side, the outcome was certainly not guaranteed. It took a solitary Duncan Edwards goal to separate the two teams.

The quarter-finals produced yet another testing tie and possible banana skin in the shape of Bournemouth and Boscombe Athletic from the Third Division South. In a closely fought encounter United managed to scrape through by the odd goal in three, throwing them into a semi-final tie against Birmingham City. Played at Hillsborough, Sheffield, there was never any doubt as to the outcome of those particular 90 minutes, with United enjoying a comfortable 2–0 victory. And so it was off to Wembley Stadium on Saturday 4 May where Aston Villa awaited, as did the possibility of making history as the first team to win the League and Cup double in 60 years.

The Birmingham side had not exactly marched to Wembley in style as they had been taken to a replay in the third round by Luton Town, eventually going through 2–0 following a 2–2 draw. Round four saw them defeat Middlesbrough 3–2, while it was again an odd-goal victory, 2–1 against Bristol City, that took them into the quarter-finals. Here Burnley provided some tough opposition, and it required a replay following a 1–1 draw before Villa were into the last four with a 2–0 victory. It took yet another replay before a place in the Final was secured and this time local rivals West Bromwich Albion stood in their way, holding them to a 2–2 draw before losing 1–0 in the replay.

United travelled south to their Cup Final headquarters of Hendon Hall, a short, five-minute drive from Wembley. The journey on match day was to take slightly longer, as one could imagine, especially as their coach neared the stadium and the volume of supporters began to increase. It was only now that the United players began to show a hint of nervous excitement, with Duncan Edwards bursting into song as the twin towers approached and the crowds became more dense, singing his own version of a popular song of the time: 'I never felt more

Matt Busby leads the United team out onto the Wembly pitch.

like running away...' The police had also to force a passage through the crowd to enable United to reach the access to the dressing-room area.

The stage was set, and at 2.52pm Roger Byrne led his white-shirted teammates from the south dressing room and out into the Wembley sunshine behind manager Matt Busby. At arms-length were their Villa opponents, also wearing their alternative shirts of light blue with a thin claret strip due to the similarity in the usual colours of both sides. United, with an average age of just 22, were the youngest-ever Cup Final team.

After both teams had been presented to the Duke of Edinburgh, Tommy Taylor got the game under way with the usual cat-and-mouse exchanges materialising in the opening minutes. Both Foulkes and Taylor gave away free-kicks, which led to pressure being put on the United goal, forcing Byrne, Edwards and Blanchflower to clear their lines. But with only five minutes gone, disaster struck United.

Sewell collected the ball around eight yards outside the United area and sent over an excellent cross towards the far post. With Foulkes caught slightly out of position, McParland was allowed a free header at goal, but this was easily held by Ray Wood. Although the ball was firmly in the 'keeper's grasp, McParland continued to move forward and charged into the unsuspecting Wood, catching him on the side of his head and knocking him to the ground. The Villa man was quickly back onto his feet, but the unfortunate Wood was left motionless on the ground. Quickly onto the pitch was United trainer Tom Curry, but his magic sponge was little help as Wood was forced to leave the field on a stretcher.

Rather surprisingly, both the sports editor and John Trickett of the *Manchester Evening News* wrote, 'Attach no blame whatsoever to McParland for this disaster. It was a sheer accident – but what a tragic one.' An accident perhaps, but the Villa outside-left was totally in the wrong as Wood had the ball firmly in his grasp, and although shoulder to shoulder contact was allowed, there was never going to be anything remotely near to that happening.

With Wood being carried from the pitch Jackie Blanchflower volunteered his services as a makeshift goalkeeper, which wasn't the end of the world as the United half-back had actually played in goal for a whole 90 minutes in the 5–1 victory against Helsingborg on the close season tour of 1956. Duncan Edwards moved to centre-half, but this certainly curtailed United's attacking instincts from the middle of the park.

Despite their obvious handicap United did threaten the Villa goal on occasions, with one advance only coming to a premature end thanks to a tackle by Lynn on Charlton, the appeals for penalty being waved away by the referee.

Following his crude and completely unnecessary challenge on Wood, McParland came in for some acts of retribution from the United defence – Foulkes left the Villa man flat on his back following one mid-air challenge – as well as being constantly booed by sections of the United support for the remainder of the game.

Blanchflower showed his ability as a stand-in 'keeper by comfortably taking the ball off the head of Myrescough before setting up a United attack. Taylor nodded the ball down to Charlton, who in turn swung it out towards Johnny Berry. The winger then found Taylor, and as the Villa defence appealed for off-side the United centre moved in on goal, but just when it looked as though he was about to score he uncharacteristically over-ran the ball.

McParland shot into the side netting but United were holding on gallantly, with Blanchflower doing his utmost to keep his goal intact, snatching the ball off the head of Sewell before stopping a shot from the same player and returning the ball up-field to a teammate for yet another assault on the Villa goal.

With half an hour played, United were still battling bravely against the 11-man Villa side, Byrne and Edwards in particular standing firm in defence, but four minutes later they were unexpectedly back to full strength as a loud cheer from the United support welcomed back Ray Wood. He was, however, wearing a white out-field shirt and, to the surprise of most, took up a position wide on the left. Although looking far from fit, at least it was now 11 against 11, and the 'keeper's presence gave United something of a lift as they mounted several attacks on the Villa goal. As the half-time whistle blew it was still United who were looking more likely to score.

As the team emerged for the second half Jackie Blanchflower still wore the green goalkeeper's jersey, but United were again a man short as Wood had failed to re-emerge from the dressing rooms. This, however, did little to deter them from taking up where they had left off, and twice Tommy Taylor came close to breaking the deadlock.

Ten minutes into the second half Wood once again emerged from the tunnel and took up an out-field position as United continued to put the Villa defence under pressure. Berry passed the ball out towards Edwards, who had forsaken his defence duties and made his way into his opponent's penalty half. He mis-kicked the ball and it went out to Pegg, but the winger's shot went wide of the goal.

Jackie Blanchflower
replaced the injured
Woods in goal.

The action was soon at the opposite end, and Edwards, back on defensive duties, had to clear almost off the line as McParland's header rebounded off the upright with Blanchflower beaten. On the hour Villa should have taken the lead, as McParland pulled the makeshift United defence out of position before getting the ball to Myerscough. The Villa centre-forward was well placed in the United area with the ball at his feet, but somehow he managed to put it wide.

Slowly Villa began to creep more and more into the game, and in the 67th minute they took the lead. On the right Dixon centred into the United area, and up jumped McParland to head past Blanchflower from around 10 yards. The goal seemed to knock United back a little, and six minutes later, before they could re-organise themselves, they were 2–0 behind. Dixon again moved forward, but his shot hit the post. The United defence did have the opportunities to clear, but they hesitated and McParland wasted little time in seizing the opportunity to grab his second. It would later be revealed that the Irishman had been in an offside position when the ball came back off the post.

Wood, although obviously still in a bit of pain, did his best whenever he got the ball, and at one point he almost created a goal, beating Aldis before crossing into the Villa goalmouth. The ball, however, was plucked out of the air by Sims before any United head could reach it. The Villa goalkeeper also did well to prevent Taylor from scoring, pushing the ball over the bar for a corner after the United centre-forward had got his head to a cross from Pegg.

As the minutes slowly ticked away United forced a series of corners, and with only eight minutes remaining Pegg swung yet another into the Villa penalty area. Tommy Taylor beat everyone in the air to head the ball over the head of Sims and into the net.

Taylor scores United's goal late in the second half.

As the United players raced back to their own half, eager to get the game restarted and look for an equaliser, there was some frantic activity on the bench in an effort to get Ray Wood back into goal, with Blanchflower resuming his out-field role.

Another Pegg cross saw Taylor rise in the air, but this time his header hit the side netting and the opportunity of an equaliser was gone. It was the Villa players who were celebrating as the referee blew for full time.

In the *People*, Joe Hulme wrote, 'My verdict on one of the most thrilling Cup Finals of all time is this: Manchester United threw the match away. They waited too long before putting the injured Ray Wood back in goal. Had they made the move 15 minutes earlier, I am certain they would have got the equaliser. When the move was made, the "Babes" were all over Villa. There just wasn't enough time left for them to get that second goal.

'I know that Roger Byrne, United's captain, doesn't agree with me. "I didn't put Wood back in goal earlier because he wasn't fit enough. In fact, he should not have come back on at all," he said.

'That is one argument that will rage for years. Another is this – was Wood's injury an accident or the result of unfair play? Matt Busby has no doubts. "The charge on Wood by McParland was not in the spirit of the game," he told me. And the referee Mr Frank Coultas agrees with him. "McParland hit Wood when his feet were off the ground," he said.'

Why, then, did the referee allow the goal to stand?

Wood himself spoke of the incident at United's after-match banquet, telling a *News of the World* reporter, 'I went back onto the field in defiance of two doctors, and I certainly wasn't fit to resume in goal. The pain in my face was agonising and my vision kept coming and going. I would probably have made a proper mess of things. I wasn't fit for goal even when I took over between the posts at the end.'

United missed out on the opportunity to clinch the double, but on the day they were considered the best of the two teams and had been beaten by nothing more than bad luck and the so-called 'Wembley Hoodoo'.

Manchester United: Wood, Foulkes, Byrne, Colman, Blanchflower, Edwards, Berry, Whelan, Taylor, Charlton, Pegg.
Scorer: Taylor.
Aston Villa: Sims, Lynn, Aldis, Crowther, Dugdale, Saward, Smith, Sewell, Myerscough, Dixon, McParland.
Scorers: McParland 2.
Attendance: 100,000.

No. 20
ARSENAL V UNITED
1 February 1958

Selecting the 30 most memorable Manchester United games from the 1950s was never going to be easy, and the selection within the pages of this book will probably be debated by many. There is, however, one game in particular that would appear on every list completed in this particular decade, and that is the First Division fixture against Arsenal at Highbury on Saturday 1 February 1958.

United travelled to Highbury as reigning League champions, but six games into the second half of the 1957–58 campaign they were in fourth position with 34 points from their 27 games, only one point behind second and third-placed Preston North End and West Bromwich Albion but six behind leaders Wolverhampton Wanderers. They were, however, unbeaten in their last nine games and fielding an unchanged team for the sixth game in succession. Arsenal were to be found in mid-table with 27 points from the same number of games played.

Byrne leads the team out against Arsenal.

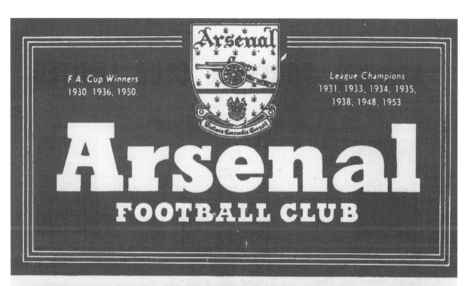

F.A. Cup Winners
1930 1936, 1950.

League Champions
1931, 1933, 1934, 1935,
1938, 1948, 1953

Arsenal

FOOTBALL CLUB

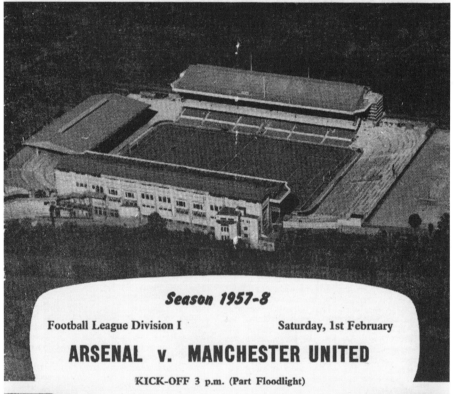

Season 1957-8

Football League Division I   Saturday, 1st February

ARSENAL v. MANCHESTER UNITED

KICK-OFF 3 p.m. (Part Floodlight)

OFFICIAL   **6d**   PROGRAMME

On the morning of the game, the United players were somewhat unsettled by the news that club director for 22 years, Mr George Whittaker, had been found dead in his hotel room. The 82-year-old was the oldest member of the board, and in a mark of respect both teams wore black arm bands as they emerged from the Highbury tunnel.

United started strongly, and as early as the opening minute Evans had to resort to unfair methods in order to stop Morgans from gaining any advantage down the right. The resulting free-kick came to nothing, and minutes later the United winger was once again in the thick of things, on this occasion scorning a good scoring opportunity by scooping the ball high over the bar.

Gregg came under a bigger threat than his goal when he made his third important save in the opening exchanges. He managed to get his hands to the ball and pulled it down to safety just as Groves came charging in towards him. Fortunately for the United 'keeper, Groves somehow managed to hurl himself over Gregg's shoulder, finishing up in the back of the net.

A Taylor shot was blocked by Kelsey and rolled towards Charlton, but as he was about to shoot, the ball was kicked off his toes and away to safety. It was inevitable that the visitors would take the lead, though, due to their almost continuous attacking play, and the breakthrough eventually came in the 10th minute.

Morgans, again a threat to the Gunners' defence, cut inside before squaring the ball to Edwards. The big wing-half hit the ball from all of 25 yards, and it flew along the ground past the outstretched fingers of Jack Kelsey and into the Arsenal net.

With United dictating play, another Edwards effort, this time, however, only half hit, went out for a corner, while a free-kick from the same player after Charlton had been badly fouled by Fotheringham went just wide of the post as Kelsey scrambled across his goal.

At the other end Gregg had to race out of his area to kick clear as Herd, having looked suspiciously off-side, raced after the ball, but despite their odd attacks the Arsenal forwards seemed to be lacking in the ability to finish the moves off. Byrne had to be alert to the danger with perfectly timed interceptions on two occasions. Jones also had to be aware of the danger of Arsenal attacks, moving quickly to take the ball off the foot of Tapscott.

Despite enjoying the majority of the play, it wasn't until the 34th minute that United scored a second goal. Gregg did well to save headers from Tapscott and Groves, and it was from his clearance from the latter that the goal came. Scanlon, who was possibly enjoying his best game for United, gained possession just inside his own half and raced down the wing past Stan Charlton, the Arsenal full-back. His precise centre picked out Bobby Charlton, and before Kelsey in the Arsenal goal could move, the ball was nestling in the back of the net.

Harry Gregg.

Four minutes from the interval Arsenal thought they had pulled a goal back, but Tapscott was adjudged to be offside. From the free-kick United raced up-field and Charlton's shot beat Kelsey, but Evans, standing on the goalline, seemed to use both his head and his hand to keep the ball out of the net. United's cries for penalty were dismissed by the referee after consultation with his linesman, and they had to be content with nothing more than a corner.

Despite the obvious relief of the Arsenal players, they were soon to find themselves three goals behind. Kelsey had done well to prevent a third, diving to save a header from Viollet, but with the referee looking at his watch and about to blow for half-time Morgans, having a field day, got the ball inside towards Taylor, and although the centre's initial shot seemed to hit Kelsey, the United number nine was onto the ball in a flash and forced it over the line. Relief was clearly written across the face of the United centre-forward as he made his way back to the centre circle amid the congratulations of his teammates because this was his first goal in seven games.

The watching Red Star Belgrade officials must have been left more than a little concerned by the brilliance of United's play, wondering how their team could hope to compete when the two sides were to meet in the European Cup quarter-final tie in a few days time, while 21-year-old Gerry Ward, playing in the Arsenal first team for only the first time in four years, could only reflect as to why his manager had to pick this particular game to throw him back into First Division action.

In the gloom of the late London afternoon even the Arsenal supporters applauded United from the field, but within 15 minutes of the restart their applause was totally reserved for their own heroes as they completely turned the game on its head with three goals in just as many minutes.

As play resumed, Edwards did well to break up an Arsenal attack, and as action swung to the opposite end and Colman and Taylor moved forward, it took something of a heavy tackle from Evans on Morgans to prevent the United winger from making the space required to get a cross into the Arsenal area.

In the 13th minute of the second half, having switched around the right-wing partnership of Groves and Tapscott, Arsenal scored, David Herd converting a cross from Groves. Groves himself almost made it two, his shot beating the unsighted Gregg, but it flashed past the outside of the post.

On the hour Arsenal had pulled it back to 3–2, with Groves again the supplier, flicking the ball through to Bloomfield, who steered it past Gregg, who tried in vain to prevent the ball from crossing the line.

One minute later the crowd went wild as the astonishing transformation was completed when the home side equalised, Bloomfield racing through the United defence on his own before smacking the ball in off the post.

United, who had been cruising at 3–0, now found themselves with a real fight on their hands and the possibility of losing the game altogether. Fighting of a different kind broke out in the Main Stand, and police and stewards had to be called in to deal with a great commotion as rival supporters began throwing punches. All eyes, however, were soon back towards the pitch, where Byrne picked up a knock following yet another desperate clearance as Arsenal continued to press forward.

Four minutes after Arsenal had grabbed the equaliser, the visitors managed to regain their lead. Scanlon, who had been neglected for much of the second half, raced down the wing, got past Arsenal full-back Charlton before sending over a superb cross to where Viollet was waiting, and his header flashed past Kelsey, who flapped helplessly at the ball as it flew into the net.

Arsenal, in the hope of penetrating the United defence, began thumping long balls forward, a move that clearly caused some concern in their defence. But they weathered the storm, and after Gregg had pulled off a brilliant save, diving at the feet of the incoming Groves, his clearance found its way to Morgans, who cleverly beat a defender before switching the ball to Taylor. The United number nine manoeuvred his way round Evans and from something of an acute angle beat Kelsey. In spite of getting his hand to the ball, it spun away from him and into the far corner of the net.

5–3 with 16 minutes remaining and the game could still swing either way. When Arsenal pulled it back to 5–4 in the 77th minute through Tapscott, the game was set for a rousing finale. Having witnessed six goals in 18 minutes, no one on the packed terracing dared move in fear of missing something in this compelling encounter.

Viollet almost notched a sixth for United when he switched positions with Morgans and got the better of Kelsey with a centre, but as the ball rolled tantalisingly towards goal Fotheringham ran in and managed to clear the ball at the expense of a corner.

There were to be no further goals, and at the final whistle the crowd stood as one, applauding both sets of players as they left the field together. As the white-shirted United players disappeared down the Highbury tunnel, little did those present realise that they had not only witnessed a game that would live in the memory forever but that it would be the last time that many who had entertained them would be seen on a Football League ground.

The newspapers of the following Sunday and Monday were full of praise for the performance of both teams, with Frank Butler in the *News of the World* writing under the heading of 'United Super Display', 'I have never seen Manchester United greater, and I haven't seen such superb fighting spirit in an Arsenal team for many seasons. All the 63,000 spectators at Highbury will agree that this was a match to remember for a long long time.'

Joe Hulme in the *People* penned the following: 'I've seen a few exciting games in my time, but by golly, this one gets into the Final. What can you do but praise a side that, by sheer good football, thumps away to three-goal lead, as Manchester United did? And what can you do but cheer a side who hit back to equalise with three goals in four minutes – as Arsenal did. After that, you've got to admire United because they didn't go to pieces. They didn't panic. They just banged in two more goals.'

It wasn't all praise for United, however, with W. Capel Kirkby in the *Empire News and Sunday Chronicle* writing, 'Manchester United had some of the cockiness taken out of them in some of the most amazing second-half football I have ever seen from an Arsenal side, or any other side in years. United should profit from this lesson. Good as they are, they cannot afford to take any opposition lightly.'

David Herd, the player who scored the first goal of the fight back, who was to sign for United a few years, said, 'I certainly would not have described them as cocky. They simply radiated confidence in their obvious ability.'

One player more than involved in this pulsating encounter was Arsenal goalkeeper Jack Kelsey, and a number of years ago the author spoke to Jack while researching his biography of Duncan Edwards. He offered the following observation and also spoke of an incident that could have resulted in an entirely different outcome for player, club and country. 'The game,' Jack began, 'was played on an exceptionally muddy surface with driving rain, and Duncan's strength and powerful frame stood out like a beacon in these conditions. After only 10 minutes he unleashed a drive from the edge of the penalty area and the ball hit the back of the net before I could move.

'During the game Duncan tackled our winger, Danny Clapton, with such power that Danny finished up spreadeagled across the running track. Our full-back, Denis Evans, whose power might have been on a par with Duncan's, went up to Duncan and suggested he cut out the tough stuff.

'Later in the match Duncan bore down on Evans and pushed the ball past him. As Duncan went by, Evans said later the thought came into his head to clobber him, and had he done so Duncan might have received an injury that would have prevented him making the trip to Belgrade. A simple incident that might have changed the course of history.'

Perhaps later Evans did regret not making that tackle, but in an age when fair play was common he didn't, and Duncan made the trip along with his teammates.

Sadly, most of the team's fine attacking play, silky skills and determined attitude would never be seen again, but the game at Highbury was a fitting memorial to Busby's team and became the benchmark of all future United sides.

Arsenal: Kelsey, S. Charlton, Evans, Ward, Fotheringham, Bowen, Groves, Tapscott, Herd, Bloomfield, Nutt.
Scorers: Herd, Bloomfield 2.
Manchester United: Gregg, Foulkes, Byrne, Colman, Jones, Edwards, Morgans, B. Charlton, Taylor, Viollet, Scanlon.
Scorers: Edwards, Charlton, Taylor 2, Viollet.
Attendance: 63,578.

No. 21

UNITED V SHEFFIELD WEDNESDAY
19 February 1958

Originally scheduled for Saturday 15 February, the events of Munich saw United given time to reassess their playing staff and have some sort of proper preparations for their fifth-round FA Cup tie against Sheffield Wednesday at Old Trafford.

Five days prior to the rearranged game United put the remaining tickets on sale. Sales that had been taking place when news of the disaster at Munich had began to filter through had been immediately abandoned. Although the much-sought-after tickets were not due to go on sale until 10am that Sunday morning, supporters began arriving at the ground around midnight. By morning countless others had made their way across the city and indeed from other parts of Lancashire, desperate to get their hands on a ticket for that all-important Cup tie, with the queue stretching round the ground and back across the Warwick Road railway bridge. Warwick Road itself was brought to a standstill, and it took police reinforcements 10 minutes to get the traffic moving again

Mounted police helped control the half-mile-long, six-deep queues, and because of the numbers, estimated at 20,000, the ticket office opened at 9am, an hour earlier than planned. Although the sale of the 15,000 tickets was restricted to one per person, they were sold out within four hours, leaving many disappointed. Some youngsters did manage to evade the scrutiny of the mounted police and made several visits to the ticket office window to purchase the all-important pieces of paper, which were quickly resold at double the price.

For those without tickets but fortunate enough to have access to a television, their hopes of catching some of the action on their screens looked to have been dashed when Football League officials expressed strong feelings against any pictures being shown on the BBC's *Sportsview* programme while the match was still in progress.

The programme would have been running as the match was being played, and the BBC announced that they would be broadcasting a 'special report' on the game. No one, however,

UNITED WILL GO ON . . .

> On 6th February, 1958 an aircraft returning from Belgrade crashed at Munich Airport. Of the twenty-one passengers who died twelve were players and officials of the Manchester United Football Club. Many others lie injured.

It is the sad duty of we who serve United to offer the bereaved our heartfelt sympathy and condolences. Here is a tragedy which will sadden us for years to come, but in this we are not alone. An unprecedented blow to British football has touched the hearts of millions and we express our deep gratitude to the many who have sent messages of sympathy and floral tributes. Wherever football is played United is mourned, but we rejoice that many of our party have been spared and wish them a speedy and complete recovery. Words are inadequate to describe our thanks and appreciation of the truly magnificent work of the surgeons and nurses of the Rechts der Isar Hospital at Munich. But for their superb skill and deep compassion our casualties must have been greater. To Professor Georg Maurer, Chief Surgeon, we offer our eternal gratitude.

> Although we mourn our dead and grieve for our wounded we believe that great days are not done for us. The sympathy and encouragement of the football world and particularly of our supporters will justify and inspire us. The road back may be long and hard but with the memory of those who died at Munich, of their stirring achievements and wonderful sportsmanship ever with us, Manchester United will rise again.

H. P. HARDMAN, CHAIRMAN

The team emerge from the tunnel at the start of the game against Sheffield Wednesday.

was certain as to what this would actually be. Speculation varied between camera shots of the crowd and/or a brief glimpse of the play itself. With other games being played at the same time, it was thought that even five minutes of action from Old Trafford being shown on television would have some adverse effect on attendances.

Jimmy Murphy had taken his collection of 19 United players, including his new £7,000 signing Ernie Taylor, to Blackpool's Norbreck Hydro Hotel (a short drive from Taylor's seaside home), away from the still grief-stricken city now beset by Cup-fever, where unscrupulous touts were asking £1 for their 6s 6d (32p) tickets. They didn't return until shortly before kick-off. As the coach rattled its way back to Manchester, Murphy decided on 10 of his 11 starting line up.

Such was the uncertainty of Murphy's selection that the printers of the club programme, the *United Review*, could only print 11 blank spaces where the names of the players should have been, with those at the match on the night having to fill in the names of those selected for themselves.

Ernie Taylor.

Stan Crowther was a late edition to the squad from Aston Villa.

The final space on Jimmy Murphy's scribbled list of names was reserved in the hope that he could bring in a late addition, Aston Villa's Stan Crowther. The in-demand half-back had travelled to Villa Park early that Wednesday morning and had spoken to his manager before taking a telephone call from Jimmy Murphy. Nothing was sorted out during the brief call, but it was agreed that the player and his manager would drive to Manchester that afternoon for further talks with the United assistant manager. Even if a deal could be struck, there was still the possibility that the FA would refuse United permission to field the player against Sheffield Wednesday.

Much to the Welshman's relief, Crowther agreed to sign and permission was granted by the Football Association. Murphy had his 11 players, and United were now set to take those first tentative steps back.

At around 7.25pm, from the mouth of the tunnel below the Main Stand, a volley of camera flash-bulbs silhouetted Bill Foulkes as he ran out in front of his fellow teammates, veering to the right towards the Warwick Road end of the ground, the section of the field where United always warmed up.

Even for the most seasoned professional within the Wednesday ranks it was difficult to focus on the game that began to unfold, but it was actually United who showed the early nerves, with the visitors enjoying the best of the opening exchanges. Three times they came close to actually scoring, and undoubtedly if any of those attempts had beaten Harry Gregg then the outcome would have been so much different.

Centre-forward Johnson sent a long-range effort wide before Gregg saved from Cargill. The big goalkeeper was beaten by a Wilkinson header but was relieved to see Ronnie Cope head the ball off the line.

Attacking the Warwick Road end, United slowly began to get their game together, growing in confidence, with Ernie Taylor seemingly involved in everything, causing Wednesday all sorts of problems. One minute he was sending Webster away on the right, the next he was swinging the ball to the opposite flank

Alex Dawson.

and into the path of the on-running Brennan. There were also through balls down the centre for either Dawson or Pearson to pursue. He even had time to have a shot at goal, his 25-yard effort through a crowd of players in the 22nd minute rebounding off the post.

Play swung from end to end, and even Bill Foulkes could be found pushing forward in search of that important opening goal, with a header from the United defender being punched round the post by Ryalls in the Wednesday goal.

From his corner-kick over on the United Road side of the ground, Shay Brennan cunningly curled the ball goalwards, and as Ryalls grasped at the cold Manchester evening air, the ball dipped below the cross-bar and into the vacant net.

It was 7.58pm. Manchester United were reborn, and the capacity crowd of 59,848 greeted the breakthrough with ear-splitting noise. It was welcomed just as loudly outside the ground by those who had been unable to obtain tickets but who simply wanted to be there, imagining and listening to the drama unfolding behind the red brick walls.

In later years Shay Brennan looked back at his defining moment in United's history and recalled, 'I went to take the corner and tried for an in-swinger by hitting the ball with my right foot. It swung beautifully under the glaring floodlights, wafted further towards goal by a gust of wind and curled over the 'keeper's head into the net.'

'It was a strange goal in many ways,' recalled George Watson, a spectator at the game. 'The ball seemed to hang in the air for a moment, and as the Wednesday goalkeeper jumped to grasp it, it dropped over his outstretched arms. You seemed to get the impression that the crowd behind the goal had sucked the ball into the net.

'There was silence for just a split second before the stadium erupted. Hats and scarves flew into the air, many never to be seen by their owners again, but who cared? There were tears too, as never before could a solitary goal have meant so much to so many.'

Quixall was Wednesday's main threat, but the United defence stood firm against anything that came their way, although at times they did border on the unorthodox. A Crowther throw-in, which was intended for Harry Gregg, who was coaxing and cajoling his defenders through the game, fell somewhat short, and as the 'keeper had to race from his area he simply headed the ball out of touch. As the game progressed he was to make three world-class saves to keep United in the game.

In front of Ryalls, centre-half Ronnie Cope played like a man possessed. His fearlessness saw him produce crunching tackles that many would have pulled out of. On one occasion he landed in a heap on top of a crowd of photographers, and on another he skidded into the barricades alongside the goal. Johnson, the Wednesday number nine, rarely got a look in.

The pace of the game was immediately picked up as the second half swung into action. Ryalls managed to punch away a threatening cross from Webster, while at the opposite end Greaves was able to kick a Wilkinson shot off the goalline before Gregg did well to hold a powerful drive from Johnson.

Following series of concentrated attacks, United scored a second goal 25 minutes into the second half. Ernie Taylor, always a problem for the Wednesday side, found Pearson out wide on the left, but the inside-forward's shot from outside the penalty area cannoned off Ryall's leg. The ball, however, rebounded only as far as Brennan, who drove the ball home with his right

Shay Brennan.

foot from 10 yards out. The youngster was engulfed in a sea of red shirts, and the noise that greeted the goal must have been heard in Manchester city centre.

Wednesday were now demolished, demoralised by this makeshift United side, and were left with no hope whatsoever of a comeback.

Gregg leapt into air to clutch a swerving corner from Cargill as it flew towards the top corner of his goal, but the majority of the action was in the opposite half of the field. Webster sent a terrific shot inches wide as United continued to press forward, and with only six minutes remaining the visitors found themselves beaten for a third time.

It was Taylor again, this time sending Pearson through, with the youngster cutting the ball back from the byline for Dawson to slam home United's third of the night with a low, hard drive that left Ryall's helpless.

To say that Ernie Taylor was inspiring is simplifying the player's contribution to the game and to United's ultimate revival. From the opening whistle he coaxed and urged the raw United recruits into action, supplying his teammates with a never-ending supply of passes, ranging from the short ball to the 20 or 30-yard cross-field ball with pin-point accuracy.

But what of Sheffield Wednesday? They were always on a hiding to nothing, and although they were superior in experience they were simply not good enough to compete against the strong-willed and ambitious United side on the night. At no point was there any sympathy in their play, as they certainly tried to compete, but at the end of the day they were beaten for skill, strength and, above all, team work.

In the aftermath of an incredible 90 minutes, which could not have been scripted by any Hollywood screen mogul, there were countless tears shed in the confines of the United dressing room — tears of joy, tears of relief and tears for those whose red shirts the team now wore.

Bill Foulkes wept unashamedly, having made his way up the tunnel to the dressing rooms. 'The lads played their hearts out,' he said, 'They couldn't have given more. I like to think they did it all for our colleagues who died at Munich. I have never cried since I was a kid, but I cried tonight. As soon as I got back to the dressing room it affected me.

'It was wonderful to be skipper of such a grand side. They fought every inch of the way and no one can say we didn't deserve our win.'

Inside the packed United dressing room, Shay Brennan gave his first post-match interview, telling the reporters as he pulled off his mud-splattered shirt, 'I never thought it would finish up like this. I was terrified before I went on the field, but once I kicked the ball and found my feet I was ok. From then on I forgot the crowd and played like any other game.'

Brennan had been the undisputed man of the match, but the victory was mainly due to the tireless work of one man, a man who had spent many a long night debating the ability of the players at his disposal, selecting countless team formations in his head before deciding on his final line-up. The night belonged to United and Shay Brennan, but it was all down to Jimmy Murphy at the end of the day.

This, however, was only the first step on a long and winding road. The 1955–56 and 1956–57 League Championship flag once again flew at full-mast high above the Old Trafford stands.

Manchester United: Gregg, Foulkes, Greaves, Goodwin, Cope, Crowther, Webster, Taylor, Dawson, Pearson, Brennan.
Scorers: Brennan 2, Dawson.
Sheffield Wednesday: Ryalls, Martin, Baker, Kay, Swan, O'Donnell, Wilkinson, Quixall, Johnson, Froggatt, Cargill.
Attendance: 59,848.

No. 22
UNITED V WEST BROMWICH ALBION
5 March 1958

Having overcome Sheffield Wednesday in round five of the 1957–58 FA Cup, United were drawn away to West Bromwich Albion in the quarter-final. After managing a 1–1 draw against Nottingham Forest at Old Trafford in what was the resumption of their First Division programme, there was certainly confidence within the team, and it was a confidence that almost took them through to the semi-finals, as it was not until the 86th minute that the home side were able to secure an Old Trafford replay with a 2–2 draw.

There were only five minutes on the clock at The Hawthorns when United opened the scoring. Ernie Taylor pushed the ball out wide to Dawson, whose cross found Charlton. It could have been a dream return to action for the lad from Ashington, but his shot was blocked by Howe. The ball wasn't cleared, however, and in stepped Taylor to fire United into the lead.

The United contingent in the 58,250 crowd, estimated at between 14 and 15,000, went wild, but their celebrations were muted when Derek Kevan broke through. His centre beat Harry Gregg, though it was also too powerful for any of his Albion teammates. Those Mancunians on the packed terracings, however, were well and truly silenced within five minutes, when Albion drew level.

Kevan was again the threat, and his powerful drive was only parried by Gregg. In the scramble that ensued, Allen managed to get to the ball and shot past the unsighted United 'keeper.

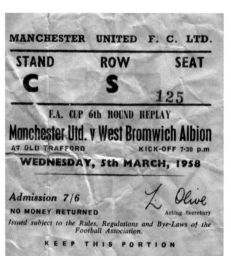

MANCHESTER UNITED F. C. LTD.

STAND ROW SEAT

C S

125

F.A. CUP 6th ROUND REPLAY

Manchester Utd. v West Bromwich Albion

AT OLD TRAFFORD   KICK-OFF 7-30 p.m

WEDNESDAY, 5th MARCH, 1958

Admission 7/6   L. Olive

NO MONEY RETURNED   Acting Secretary

Issued subject to the Rules, Regulations and Bye-Laws of the Football Association.

KEEP THIS PORTION

Play was fast and furious, with the United youngsters keeping their more experienced opponents stretched to their limits and unable to play the type of football that had taken them to third place in the First Division.

With three minutes remaining before the interval, the visitors regained their lead thanks again to the sterling work of their midfield general, Ernie Taylor. The former Blackpool man was the inspiration behind United's rebuilding, and had it not been for

MANCHESTER
UNITED
FOOTBALL CLUB

UNITED REVIEW

MANCHESTER
UNITED
v
W. BROMWICH
ALBION
Kick-off 7-30 pm

1957-58

SEASON

5th March

4d.

NUMBER 23
(F.A. CUP, 6th ROUND
REPLAY)

OFFICIAL

PROGRAMME

A *Manchester Evening News* Photo

UNITED WILL GO ON...

him, not just in this important Cup tie but throughout the remainder of this campaign, then things could have been so much different.

Moments before the goal Taylor had wriggled his way past a static-looking Albion defence and sent Dawson through on goal. The burly centre-forward, however, shot wildly over the bar when he should have done much better. In their next attack Dawson certainly redeemed himself, rising to head the ball firmly past Sanders in the West Bromwich goal after Taylor's 25-yard drive rebounded off the crossbar.

With half-time beckoning, United had a huge let-off as Kevan ran through with only Gregg to beat, but from 10 yards out he could only watch in anguish as his shot rebounded off the post.

The second pulsating 45 minutes was certainly not for the faint-hearted, with the United defence standing firm as Albion surged forward time and time again, but they could not find any way through.

Leaving themselves exposed due to their seemingly constant attacks in search of the equaliser, United were always a danger, and Pearson should have put the game beyond any doubts late on, but he blazed the ball over the top of an open goal.

Slowly Albion's experience and constant attacking began to take its toll on United, and with only four minutes remaining Ronnie Allen pounced on a loose ball to volley goalwards. Gregg, for the first time in the match, failed to hold the ball, and in stepped Horobin to slip the ball towards the net. Gregg reacted quickly and dived again for the ball, scooping it away with the help of Cope.

Without hesitation the referee awarded a goal, and hundreds of schoolboys quickly invaded the pitch, thinking that it was full-time, as the United players protested that the ball had not crossed the line. In his disagreement, Gregg threw his glove at the official but escaped a caution, and a couple of minutes later the whistle sounded the end of the match.

Afterwards, the disappointed United goalkeeper admitted that the ball had indeed crossed the line. 'The ball hit me on the leg and rolled toward goal. Ronnie Cope scooped it clear, but it had been over the line all right. The tension and excitement made me appeal. It was a terrible thing to happen with us so close to winning.'

Manager Jimmy Murphy had no real complaints. 'On the run of the play and abilities of the teams, I think a draw was correct. Every player did his part nobly. That is good enough for me.'

Hopes were still high that a place in the last four would be obtained, but it was not a view shared by everyone and not just those from the Midlands. Terence Elliott of the *Daily Express* put his head on the block by stating, 'I Must Pick Albion,' but was also quick to point out that he would be just as happy if he was to be proved wrong. He wrote, 'I think Manchester United's interest in the FA Cup will end tonight under the Old Trafford lights. To win, United must miraculously find another untapped source of physical strength and stamina.'

Fellow journalist Keith Dewhurst of the *Manchester Evening Chronicle* was equally uncertain of the outcome. 'If the issue is still undecided at about the 70th minute, or if the game goes into extra time, I fear that West Brom will pull out that little bit extra and win.'

Defeat was not part of Jimmy Murphy's vocabulary, and he pondered long and hard with his team selection for the West Bromwich replay. Many thought that he would leave out Colin Webster, who had not shown the form that he was capable of producing over the past three games, with recent recruit Warren Bradley tipped as his possible replacement.

As it turned out Murphy did make a change to his selected 11, but it was the experienced Stan Crowther who was omitted, not Webster. The former Villa player was left on the sidelines with a heel injury, forcing the stand-in manager to bring in 20-year-old Bobby Harrop at left-half for his first-team debut. The actual severity of United's situation and the problems surrounding Jimmy Murphy were again highlighted with Harrop's selection, as the former Wolves amateur had been playing mainly at inside-left and had even turned out for the reserves at centre-forward the previously Saturday.

For those who attended the Sheffield Wednesday Cup tie, the absorbing 90 minutes of football and the evening as a whole would be etched forever into the memory. The same could also be said for those who ventured to Old Trafford on the evening of 5 March, but for many they would narrate a completely different story to that surrounding the previous round. The 90 minutes were possibly on par to those of the Sheffield Wednesday match, but the scenes outside the ground were as unforgettable as those played out on the opposite side of the red brick wall, and not for the first time in recent weeks did the name 'Manchester United' appear on the front pages of the national press as well as the back.

'90,000 in Cup Storm – Locked Out Fans Miss Last-Minute Victory' proclaimed the *Daily Express*, while 'Chaos for a Mile Around Manchester United Ground' appeared on the front of the *News Chronicle and Daily Despatch*.

Beneath the *Express* headlines, a photograph, taken outside the ground prior to the game, showed little more than a sea of heads, with the caption beneath reading, 'Still an hour to kick-off last night, the gates are shut and 60,000 are INSIDE Old Trafford. But OUTSIDE – a milling 30,000 crowd…turned away.'

By 6.25pm the gates were firmly locked as late-comers, including West Bromwich Albion supporters, pushed frantically forward in the hope of making the turnstiles, having picked up tickets from the touts who were doing a brisk trade in selling 7s 6d (38p) stand tickets for £7. Some never even managed to get within sight of the ground as announcements were made at Central Station informing them that the gates had been closed and that there would be no more trains running. Strangely, many decided to make their way to Maine Road to watch City play Birmingham City!

A number of youngsters tried to gain access to the ground by scaling the walls but were unceremoniously pulled down by police officers and led away, creating unwanted scenes of objects being thrown in the direction of the police. As three mounted officers attempted to regain some form of control, one was almost pulled from his saddle. The attention was then turned to the locked gates and two were pulled off their hinges, but those hoping for entry were repelled by a wall of policemen standing shoulder-to-shoulder inside the ground.

Chief Superintendent Frederick Waddington, head of the Manchester Division of the Lancashire County police said, 'In 22 years controlling crowds at Old Trafford I have never seen

137

anything like it. My officers tell me the trouble was caused by youths and a few hotheads. There was no need for drastic action and all of the men, I believe, handled themselves extremely well in what could have been difficult circumstances.'

Unaware of the unfolding drama outside, Murphy prepared his troops for the battle ahead, but even he was not ready for the early onslaught from his former team as Albion pushed forward from the first whistle, shooting at sight but finding Harry Gregg in superb form.

The visitors forced Gregg into action four times in as many minutes as the game got under way, but it was that all-round confidence that helped United gain the advantage as early as the fifth minute when Ernie Taylor opened the scoring, having begun the move that also involved Dawson and Charlton, the latter's shot being blocked before the inside-forward stepped in to score.

Bobby Harrop was not slow in moving up in support of his forwards, and on one occasion, when sent through by Charlton, he saw his drive hit Kennedy on the arm, creating frantic appeals for a penalty. The referee correctly waved those appeals away and allowed play to continue, but the ball was soon back in the Albion penalty area. On this occasion it was scrambled away after Dawson's header had hit Saunders.

Amid the rather frantic opening, with Albion involved as much as United, Gregg was forced to pull off a superb save in the 12th minute from Bobby Robson, and it was not until mid-way through the half that play seemed to settle down, with both defences clearly on top and tackles often not for cowards. The referee had to speak to Mark Pearson on one occasion, while Kennedy brought down Taylor rather forcefully on the edge of the Albion penalty area. The referee, however, seemed quite content to stand back and let both sides literally fight it out.

United almost made the sought-after breakthrough seven minutes before half-time when Dawson shot against an Albion defender, and then Charlton seized the rebound and smashed the ball towards goal, only to see Saunders in the Albion net get his fingertips to the ball, pushing it onto the post, before watching it bounce to safety.

United slowly found their feet, with Cope and Harrop gradually coming to grips with the thrusting Albion attacks. Charlton left the imprint of the ball on the foot of the post in the 38th minute, but it wasn't until the opening 10 minutes of the second half that they came close to breaching the visitors' defence and breaking the deadlock, with Taylor, Goodwin and Dawson all coming close. Albion, however, failed to succumb, and the trio of Barlow, Kevan and Robson pushed United to the limits.

Having reshuffled his forward line continuously throughout the match, Charlton and Webster moving inside, Pearson and Taylor going wide, Murphy, looking at his watch, sensed that it was now or never as there was little more remaining than a minute plus any stoppage time that the referee felt like adding on. He quickly left his seat and made his way down to the touchline, where he shouted to trainer Jack Crompton, 'Now, Jack, now.' Knowing what was required, Crompton immediately caught the attention of Charlton, telling him to switch with Webster.

Almost immediately, Foulkes shouldered Horobin off the ball before dispatching it somewhat unstylishly down the wing towards Charlton. Albion centre-half Kennedy attempted

Colin Webster (right) touches home a perfect Bobby Charlton cross in the last minute of their Old Trafford replay against West Bromwich Albion.

Colin Webster.

to bundle the Munich survivor off the ball, but as the linesman's flag fluttered in the cold evening air the referee allowed play to continue and, having found the necessary space, Charlton also avoided Williams before crossing the ball towards the feet of the on-running Webster, who repaid his manager's faith in him by side-footing the ball past the helpless Sanders from two yards out.

A deafening roar thundered through the night air as the referee signalled full time, with trainer Jack Crompton sprinting from his touchline post, making a beeline for Colin Webster. He lifted him off his feet and kissed him firmly on the cheek before congratulating the rest of the mud-stained, red-shirted heroes.

As the champagne corks popped in the dressing room, Bill Foulkes said, 'This was the toughest game of them all. Now we have achieved the impossible, and I can tell you plainly that we at Old Trafford fancy our chances for the Cup. Footballers never try to count their chickens before they are hatched, and I would not be so foolish as to say we shall win the Cup – or even get to Wembley. But we have a good chance, and any other Cup club who have other ideas had better be prepared for a hard fight.'

For the hero of the hour, Colin Webster, who had come in for some rather unjust criticism prior to the game, scoring the only goal was a much-needed confidence boost, and he confessed to 'being in a whirl ever since I saw the ball go into the net. Although it was only from three yards' range, it was a strain at the time. But it all looked so easy on TV.'

It wasn't only in Manchester that there were celebrations following the dramatic Cup victory. There was also jubilation hundreds of miles away in Munich as the match was broadcast to those survivors still in hospital, with Chairman Harold Hardman making a telephone call to Ray Wood minutes after the final whistle.

Manchester United: Gregg, Foulkes, Greaves, Goodwin, Cope, Harrop, Webster, Taylor, Dawson, Pearson, Charlton.
Scorer: Webster.
West Bromwich Albion: Saunders, Howe, Williams, Dudley, Kennedy, Barlow, Whitehouse, Robson, Allen, Kevan, Horobin.
Attendance: 60,000.

No. 23

FULHAM V UNITED

26 March 1958

Cup semi-finals can be tense, unremarkable cat-and-mouse affairs, mainly due to the fact that there is so much at stake, but the 1958 Villa Park meeting between United and Fulham produced a four-goal thriller, although Frank McGhee of the *Daily Mirror* reckoned that it was United's 'worst display since Munich'.

Bobby Charlton put United in front after only 12 minutes with a goal that was soon to become something of a trademark, firing home on the half-volley from 20 yards out, Macedo in the Fulham goal barely moving.

Fulham equalised immediately from the restart, Stevens prodding the ball over the line from close range after Langley's run down the wing created the opening, and seven minutes before half-time they were in front through Jimmy Hill, who charged past Cope before beating the advancing Gregg, with Fulham having dictated most of the play since drawing level.

Langley, the Fulham left-back, was injured just before the interval, and with their opponents reduced to 10 men, United made the most of their advantage. Bobby Charlton pushed United in front in the time added on for Langley's injury, latching on to a rebound that left him with little else to do but score.

Fulham never looked the same following Langley's injury and many thought that United would run out winners, but, to their credit, the Craven Cottage side battled away and kept danger-man Bobby Charlton at bay. Macedo produced two world-class saves from the United forward, while 10 minutes from time it was the cross-bar that came to their rescue when Charlton's drive rattled against it.

The replay was scheduled for Arsenal's Highbury Stadium, with United voicing their complaints at the

ARSENAL FOOTBALL
CLUB, LTD.
N° 367
To be retained.

ARSENAL STADIUM,
HIGHBURY, N.5.

F.A. Challenge Cup, Semi-Final Replay.
MANCHESTER UNITED
v.
FULHAM
WEDNESDAY, 26th MARCH, 1958
Kick off 3.0 p.m.

AVENELL ROAD
LOWER TIER
(SEATING)
GUARANTEED SEAT
UNRESERVED **10/-**

choice of venue. They protested that it was unfair that they should have to travel to London when Highbury was only a 1s 4d (less than 6p) tube ride from Craven Cottage and, aside from the team's expenses, it would cut down the level of their support because of the time and money involved. Some Fulham people pointed out that they had thought it unfair that if West Bromwich Albion had beaten United then they would have had to face them at nearby Villa Park in the first leg.

In reply the Football Association said that they had considered all the above points, but there could be no alterations to their plans, leaving the United supporters who decided to travel with the choice of two trains south, at 6.42am and 7.32am on the morning of the match, at a cost of £1 18s 3d (approximately £1.90p). Even then, there was no guarantee that they would get in, as the game was not all-ticket.

Entry to Highbury turned out to not be a problem. United's call to the FA to reconsider its selection of the venue was justified when only 38,000 clicked through the turnstiles of a ground that could comfortably hold 68,000. It was the lowest Cup semi-final crowd for 29 years, and the major reason behind the lack of interest was the decision to televise the game, but in the *News Chronicle* Ian Wooldrige also suggested that the rumours of supporters queuing since dawn helped to keep the attendance down, as many felt that it could well be a wasted journey. Some, however, did brave the cold and the rain, with a reported 200 queuing outside Highbury as early as 6am, and when the gates opened at 12.30pm there was a queue stretching some 300 yards up Highbury Hill.

Police were standing-by for vast numbers of supporters converging on the ground, but as kick-off approached, those supporters never materialised, and Arsenal secretary Bob Wall assessed the loss in revenue as around £5,000, clearly citing television as the cause. United, who would have received a cut of the actual gate money, lost around £1,250.

For those who did decide to travel to North London, they were treated to an eight-goal thriller and certainly received value for money, with John Camkin in his *News Chronicle* report writing, 'The nerves and indecision, so marked in Saturday's 2–2 draw at Villa Park, were swept away in the first 12 minutes of this critical game. Six powerful shots and five corners almost swamped Fulham.

'United, I believe, would have won without the help of unfortunate Tony Macedo, Fulham's brilliant goalkeeper. His first serious blunders in top-class football cost three first-half goals.'

United lost possession right from the kick-off and Fulham surged forward on the well-sanded pitch, with Gregg forced to race from his line in order to beat Stevens to the ball. But play quickly switched to the opposite end, and Macedo's confidence took a severe dent in those opening minutes when he fumbled a 20-yard shot from Freddie Goodwin, just managing to grab it at the second opportunity as it rolled precariously towards the line. A minute later the Fulham 'keeper was powerless and indeed fortunate as Goodwin, once again in the thick of the action, drove a rising shot against the cross-bar.

Jimmy Murphy had sprung something of a surprise on his opponents by playing Dawson, although wearing the number-nine shirt, at outside-right, with Webster moving inside, and bringing Shay Brennan back into the side at outside-left, replacing Mark Pearson, who was in the unfortunate position of finding himself dropped.

With 14 minutes gone the nervous Macedo was finally beaten as United took the lead. Fulham centre-half Stapleton pushed Webster in the back, and from the resulting free-kick United won a corner. Taking it short, Brennan passed to Webster, and for some unknown reason the Fulham 'keeper moved out from his goal in an effort to narrow the angle, but the shot he was expecting failed to materialise and, as the cross came over, Dawson nipped in unmarked from the right, his diving header flashing into the net past the outstretched hand of a helpless defender on the goalline.

Fulham weathered the storm and fought back, drawing level in the 27th minute through Stevens, who beat Gregg with a first-time shot from a Haynes pass. But seven minutes later the local side were again behind when the Dawson–Webster switch paid off, with the latter swinging the ball out to the right and the burly centre/winger suddenly switching the ball to his left foot before crashing it home from the 18-yard line when there seemed to be little danger. Macedo, perhaps slightly unsighted, allowed it to slip through his hands, mainly due to the power of the shot rather than poor goalkeeping.

It was a lead that United did not hold for long; within three minutes Fulham were again level. Always looking dangerous in their breakaways, Langley, fully recovered from his injury received in the first game, raced down the left. From his cross, as the United defence held back for some unknown reason, Chamberlain side-footed the ball past Gregg.

With two minutes remaining until half-time Ernie Taylor, having had something of a quiet game by his usual standards, suddenly sprang into action, dribbling his way through a bemused Fulham defence, beating left-half Lawler, then right-half Bentley, and centre-half Stapleton before pushing the ball through towards Dawson and Brennan. Macedo dived for the ball but failed to grasp it, presenting Brennan with the easiest of opportunities to put United in front.

As the second half got under way, Gregg, as he had done in the opening minutes of the first half, had to race from his line as Dwight ran through the middle of the United defence. Gregg smothered the ball before the Fulham forward could reach it.

Dawson then raced half the length of the field but shot wide, while at the opposite end Hill and Chamberlain tried on three occasions to force the ball over the line as Gregg lay on the ground, but even if they had succeeded the goal would not have stood because the referee blew for offside.

For United, Crowther and Goodwin in particular were in exceptional form. The former Aston Villa man was strong in defence, while Goodwin was not only an able assistant but

Ernie Taylor.

also a danger to Fulham when combining defence with attack.

Macedo saved on the line from Brennan as play swung relentlessly from end to end, but it looked all over for Fulham 11 minutes into the second half when Bobby Charlton ran down the left, waltzing past one defender after another, before passing to Dawson, who accepted the opportunity to put United 4–2 in front and complete his hat-trick.

For many lesser sides that would have signalled game over, but Fulham continued to plod away and were rewarded with a third goal in the 73rd minute. A Stevens centre from the right was chested down by Chamberlain, and as Gregg failed to reach the ball Dwight won the goalmouth scramble and dribbled round the stranded United 'keeper, sprawled on the ground, before squeezing the ball over the line. Did Fulham have enough in reserve to snatch an equaliser and perhaps force the game into extra time?

With four minutes remaining Haynes had the ball in the United net, but as the Fulham players and supporters celebrated the referee signalled a free-kick to United because he had judged that Haynes had controlled the bouncing ball with his hand before scoring.

As fog shrouded the pitch and full-time beckoned, Charlton put the game beyond any doubt when he scored United's fifth, shooting past an unsighted Macedo. Frank McGhee in the *Daily Mirror* described the result as 'the greatest Manchester United

Stan Crowther.

win of them all. This was their five-goal triumphant return to the days when Manchester United were a complete, controlled footballing outfit. This was the victory which owed nothing to hysteria from the terraces or tough desperation on the field. This was soccer science, cold and surgical and deadly. And how appropriate that they should do it at Highbury, the last League ground their great Busby Babes played on before the Munich tragedy.'

Although Macedo's goalkeeping errors had a bearing on the result, no one could deny United the glory of reaching Wembley for the second successive season, in what was only the second time that eight goals had been scored in the semi-final of the FA Cup in its 86-year history, equalling West Bromwich Albion's 6–2 victory over Nottingham Forest in 1892.

The game also conjured up a few other interesting quirks. It was the fourth year in a row that Manchester supplied one of the Wembley finalists, City having been there in 1955 and 1956. It provided Ernie Taylor with the opportunity of becoming only the second player to have played in the FA Cup Final with three different clubs, former United forward Harold Halse being the other, with United in 1909, Aston Villa in 1913 and Chelsea in 1915.

Stan Crowther now had the chance to become the only player to have won a Cup-winners' medal with two different clubs in successive seasons, while Shay Brennan and Mark Pearson could make it the third season in a row that a young professional had earned a winners' medal in his first season in senior football, Dyson of Manchester City and Stan Crowther during his time at Aston Villa being the others.

Unfortunately the record books would not be rewritten, but no one associated with Manchester United was concerned about this. The main thing was that they had reached Wembley Stadium, against all the odds, and the club had done much more than survive from the ashes of Munich.

Manchester United: Gregg, Foulkes, Greaves, Goodwin, Cope, Crowther, Webster, Taylor, Dawson, Charlton, Brennan.
Scorers: Dawson 3, Brennan, Charlton.
Fulham: Macedo, Cohen, Langley, Bentley, Stapleton, Lawler, Dwight, Hill, Stevens, Haynes, Chamberlain.
Scorers: Stevens, Chamberlain, Dwight.
Attendance: 38,258.

No. 24
UNITED V BOLTON WANDERERS
3 May 1958

Having been left disappointed beneath Wembley's twin towers some 12 months previously, there was a hint of determination at Old Trafford as 1957 ebbed away and the early days of 1958 once again brought the draw for the third round of that year's competition.

As in the previous campaign, the third-round draw took Manchester United to the ground of a lesser club and, on this particular occasion, something of a footballing outpost, with Workington welcoming their rather distinguished guests to their humble Borough Park ground.

Managed by Joe Harvey, the former Newcastle United favourite, Workington caught their illustrious visitors cold with a goal from Colbridge in the fifth minute and, if they had taken their chances, they could well have found themselves further ahead by the interval. Strangely, it wasn't until five minutes before half-time that Newlands in the home goal had to make his first save, when he turned a Viollet shot round the post.

The 1958 Cup Final team.

THE FOOTBALL ASSOCIATION CHALLENGE CUP COMPETITION

FINAL TIE
BOLTON WANDERERS
V
MANCHESTER UNITED

SATURDAY, MAY 3rd, 1958   KICK-OFF 3 pm

EMPIRE STADIUM
WEMBLEY

OFFICIAL PROGRAMME   ·   ONE SHILLING

It was Viollet who, after the interval, caused Workington the most problems and who was responsible for their hopes of making FA Cup history coming to an end with three goals in an eight-minute spell.

Under the lights Newlands saved well from both Charlton and Edwards, but in the 54th minute he could do little to stop Viollet from scoring the equaliser following a pass from Taylor. Two minutes later Viollet notched his second from a Colman centre and in the 62nd minute claimed his hat-trick, with Scanlon on this occasion the provider.

Round four brought United a much-sought-after home draw, with Ipswich Town having to make the long journey from East Anglia to the North West for a match that was in some doubt two days prior to the fixture because the Old Trafford pitch was sitting under nine inches of snow. Thanks to the efforts of ground staff and supporters the pitch was cleared and the game went ahead as planned.

United stormed the Ipswich defence straight from the kick-off and missed at least three sitters in the opening 11 minutes, and for long periods the visitors' penalty area was under a constant siege. Scanlon fired the ball across goal from eight yards in the fifth minute, and Charlton should have done better with a shot from the edge of the area and certainly should have scored from seven yards out instead of firing high over the crossbar.

It was five minutes prior to the half-time interval when United finally opened the scoring. Charlton redeemed himself for his earlier misses, giving Bailey no chance as he fired home Morgans' cross from the edge of the penalty box.

The second half was almost identical to the first, but it was not until the final five minutes that United secured victory. Charlton scored, this time taking the ball in his stride before striking it from some 20 yards out.

Having safely negotiated round four, expectations began to intensify and hopes were high that further progress would be made. The events of Munich brought such dreams to a premature halt, with the games that made up rounds five and six and the semi-final taking up the previous pages of this book. Having overcome Sheffield Wednesday amid an evening of emotion never before experienced on the ground of any other League club, then West Bromwich Albion, scraping through by a solitary goal at Old Trafford following a 2–2 draw at the Hawthorns, and finally Fulham, again after a replay, United were once again heading for Wembley with all but the support of fellow finalists and Lancastrian neighbours Bolton Wanderers willing them to succeed.

As it had been assistant manager Jimmy Murphy who had guided his makeshift United side to Wembley in the absence of Matt Busby, it was only fitting that the genial Welshman walked out into the London sunshine ahead of the 11 heroes who had achieved the impossible.

Busby was present, having joined his players for lunch before arriving half an hour prior to kick-off and being driven right into the ground via the royal tunnel entrance. Looking well, he walked to the mouth of the tunnel beneath the royal box with the aid of a specially constructed walking stick, where a wicker chair had been placed for him. While awaiting the arrival of the Duke of Edinburgh, he was met by numerous individuals who all greeted him

Ticket for the Final Tie.

warmly. Prior to kick-off he moved to a touchline seat just behind Jimmy Murphy, having declined a seat in the royal box because he felt he would be unable to climb the stairs.

Outside there was the usual pandemonium as latecomers rushed for their respective turnstiles and ticket touts did their best to tempt ticketless supporters to part with their hard-earned cash. Some, however, got more than they had bargained for, as large numbers of Bolton and United supporters staged a revolt against the touts, refusing to pay the prices asked, leaving them with handfuls of spares even after the match had started. One supporter, however, was quite happy to pay out £50 for a 50s (£2.50) ticket. Prior to the United supporters leaving Manchester, one tout had been attacked by five men outside London Road Station and robbed of four 3s 6d tickets.

There was something of a lively start to the game, with Stevens of Bolton requiring attention in the opening minutes following a challenge from behind by Crowther, but it was the white-shirted Wanderers who had the first real goal-scoring opportunity. A high ball in the United area from outside-right Birch was collected by Gregg, but, rather uncharacteristically, the goalkeeper dropped the ball. He was relieved when it went out of play rather than fall to the feet of the lurking Lofthouse.

With only three minutes gone United suddenly found themselves behind. Edwards made progress down the left and managed to thread the ball through to an unmarked Lofthouse who was hovering around the penalty spot. Before Gregg could get close enough to smother the ball or Crowther could get a tackle in, the Bolton centre had hit the ball firmly into the back of the net.

United's defence were being stretched and outplayed in those early stages, with the ball seldom seen in the Bolton half. Lofthouse found Birch in space down the right, and the ball was almost immediately dispatched to Holden on the opposite wing. His shot, however, was well blocked by Foulkes.

Crowther was certainly making his presence felt and was spoken to by the referee after another crunching tackle on Stevens, which even dislodged a couple of pieces of turf. From the resulting free-kick Gregg once again gathered the ball only to drop it, with the stuttering United defence managing to scramble the ball away to safety.

Bolton were happy to shoot on sight but United were clearly struggling, and in one rare attacking move Ernie Taylor lobbed the ball forward to Webster, who beat a defender before crossing towards Viollet. Although in a good position, the United inside man fired over. Goodwin started a move that produced another opportunity for United to level, his long pass out of defence finding Webster, who in turn passed to Viollet before Taylor forced a fine save out of Hopkinson.

At the opposite end Gregg had put his errors behind him and pulled off a couple of good saves as Bolton continued to keep pushing the United defence, but as half-time approached, United were slowly settling down and beginning to make their presence felt in the Wanderers' half.

A low shot from Charlton forced Hopkinson to his knees while Dawson, having returned to his starting position on the right after a spell on the left side, managed to force a corner. From the flag kick the diminutive Taylor managed to get his head to the ball, but it flew harmlessly over.

Despite having a pin in his shoulder from a recent injury, Lofthouse was clearly a threat to United's side and looked dangerous every time he got the ball, and within minutes of the restart he had twice come near to increasing Bolton's lead. Gregg first managed to hold a header, while another effort, after he had shook off Goodwin, went narrowly over.

Bolton's first goal against United.

Lofthouse bundles the ball and Gregg into the back of the net for Bolton's second goal.

United were still searching for a way through in order to snatch the equaliser, and they came close on a couple of occasions in the opening stages of the second half. Following neat play between Viollet, Charlton and Webster, the latter was closed down by Higgins as he prepared to shoot. Then came the most amazing escape for Bolton when a Charlton drive from the edge of the penalty area beat Hopkinson but hit the post and rebounded back into the 'keeper's arms.

Almost on the hour mark United's hope took a second knock. From just inside the left corner of the penalty area Stevens drove the ball towards goal and, because of the power behind it, all Harry Gregg could do was palm it high into the air before catching it as it came down. As he did so, Lofthouse raced in and bundled the United 'keeper and ball into the back of the net.

Bill Clarke, in the *Manchester Evening Chronicle*, wrote, 'Although the charge was rather robust, it was quite fair because Gregg was in possession. Unfortunately for United, Gregg was injured, and it was some time before he was able to resume after attention from both United and Bolton trainers.

'Gregg erred in not turning the ball over the bar. He was, in fact, a "sitting duck" for Lofthouse, who quite fairly took advantage.'

In the *Sunday Graphic*, Basil Easterbrook saw the incident as follows: 'A United player was sold a dummy to let Stevens in on the left. He let fly with every ounce of power in his lithe young body. Gregg pushed the ball up in the air. He could have flicked it over the bar, but his side were one down and he wanted the ball to belt back up field and send his forwards in search of the equaliser.

'Off balance, Gregg reached backwards and grabbed the ball. Lofthouse had the situation sized up in a trice. He raced forward, hurtled through the air and, at the very moment Gregg was making sure his grip on the ball and fighting to regain his balance, sent the goalkeeper and ball spinning between the posts.'

Following the incident, Lofthouse was loudly booed by the United support every time he touched the ball, while the burly forward later claimed, 'I headed the ball over the line as it came down and before Harry caught it.'

Gregg, on the other hand, said, 'I remember nothing of the second goal. I had to turn round to catch the ball. All I could see was the crowd. Then something hit me. I don't blame Nat, I'd have done the same.'

It was around four minutes before Harry Gregg could resume his duties between the posts, but the goal seemed to kill the game as a contest, with United struggling to gain any form of control on the proceedings. Taylor, having been much involved in the early stages, had now faded into the background, and the few opportunities that were to come United's way in the closing stages, which fell mainly to Dennis Viollet, were either blotted out by the Bolton defence, put wide or saved comfortably by Hopkinson.

Bolton now seemed content to see out the game at their own pace, with United realising that there was to be no fairytale finish to such a dramatic season, and for the second time in 12 months they would simply be remembered as FA Cup runners-up, although few could forget the events that enabled them to make that trip up Wembley Way.

In the *News of the World*, Frank Butler summed up the afternoon: 'Let me brush aside all sentiment right away and say that these happy wanderers from Bolton deserved to win. They were the more complete and sturdy side and in their captain, Nat Lofthouse, who scored both goals, they had a complete winner.

'The Busby Babes were never quite good enough, but they failed gloriously and, with just a little luck, they might have won.'

Jimmy Murphy, the chain-smoking United stand-in manager, gave his own thoughts on the outcome to Butler, saying, 'I am still very proud of the way these United boys got to Wembley and the way they performed today. But there is no question that the better team won.'

For United, it would be another five years before they graced the Wembley stage again, mainly due to the rebuilding work that was necessary for Matt Busby to carry out upon his return to something like his old self. But at least they did return and, in doing so, banished the so-called 'Wembley Hoodoo' that had brought an end to the dreams of Cup Final success in both 1957 and 1958.

Manchester United: Gregg, Foulkes, Greaves, Goodwin, Cope, Crowther, Dawson, Taylor, Charlton, Viollet, Webster.
Bolton Wanderers: Hopkinson, Hartle, Banks, Hennin, Higgins, Edwards, Birch, Stevens, Lofthouse, Parry, Holden.
Scorer: Lofthouse 2.
Attendance: 100,000.

No. 25
UNITED V AC MILAN
8 May 1958

The European Cup had only been spoken about on the odd occasion, while the subject of flying had been briefly brought up with those who had survived unscathed in Munich. When questioned on the subject, Harry Gregg was quick to say no but admitted, 'To put it bluntly, I don't want to fly. How I shall feel later, I do not know. I am not afraid of flying but what happened at Munich was terrible to see.' Bobby Charlton was of a similar opinion, saying, 'I don't fancy it yet. And Bill Foulkes feels the same.'

Chairman Harold Hardman was uncommitted as to both a mode of travel to their semi-final tie, or indeed whether the club would actually fulfil their European commitments. 'We are not keen on the prospect of long train journeys across the continent. If we draw Borussia Dortmund and Milano (the two clubs still having to play) and Borussia get through, our tie will be quite definitely on.

'If we have to go to Milan, Budapest or Madrid, I would say the chance of continuing is 50–50, but United do not plan to fly to any of the remaining European Cup games.'

Representing United at the European Cup semi-final draw in Brussels was the Scottish FA secretary, Sir George Graham, and he was given some surprising and most welcome news after he spoke to the organising committee of United's reluctance to travel by air. It was decided overwhelmingly, by both the committee and officials of the other clubs left in the competition, that the draw would be 'fixed' in United's favour.

In reality there was no actual draw as it was simply decided that United would play either Borussia Dortmund or Milan, enabling them to remain in the competition and travel to the away leg by train. It was some 640 miles to Dortmund and 1,024 miles to Milan, but both were considered accessible by rail.

United were certainly most grateful to the organisers for this tremendous gesture, but it was not something that went down well with everyone. David Jack, the former Arsenal player and now a columnist with the *Empire News and Sunday Chronicle*, who only a short while earlier had advocated that League clubs should have done more to help United,

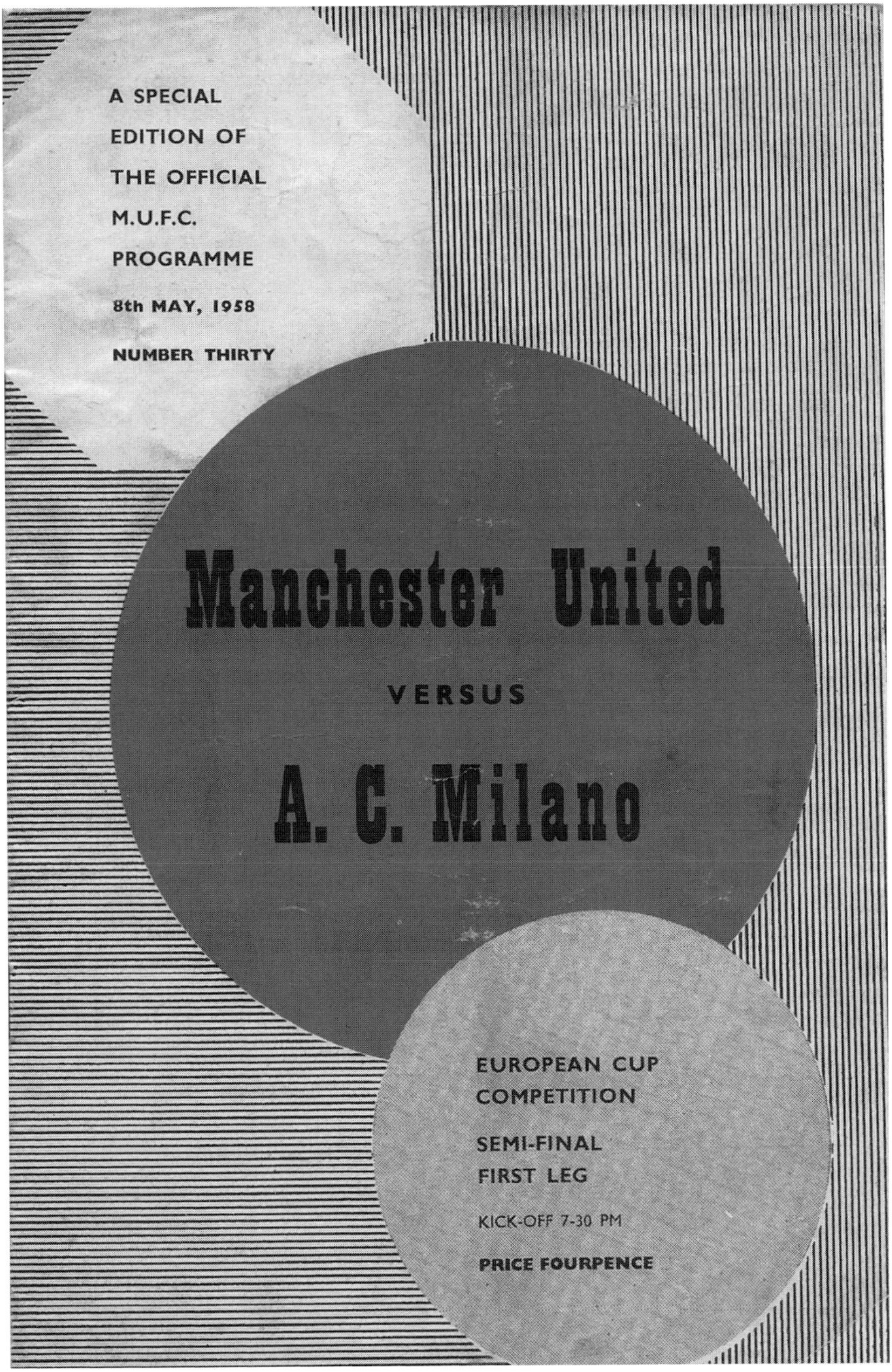

A SPECIAL
EDITION OF
THE OFFICIAL
M.U.F.C.
PROGRAMME

8th MAY, 1958

NUMBER THIRTY

Manchester United

VERSUS

A. C. Milano

EUROPEAN CUP
COMPETITION

SEMI-FINAL
FIRST LEG

KICK-OFF 7-30 PM

PRICE FOURPENCE

was stinging in his comments as far as the European Cup was concerned. 'This is carrying sentiment too far,' read the headline on his article. He went on to write that although he was in favour of helping United, he wanted to know why the rules were ignored, with only four of the five clubs agreeable because the Hungarian team of Vasas Budapest could not be contacted.

Jack felt that Real Madrid had the beating of anyone and were more than happy to play Vasas. Both Milan and Dortmund would be happy to play United – with 14 of their best 17 players no longer playing, they should be able to beat them over the two legs. As for the Hungarians, he felt that they had received a raw deal and would certainly not be happy at being allocated Real Madrid.

United and Jimmy Murphy were quick to point out that they had not looked for any favours and would have happily taken a straight draw, but they certainly appreciated the 'wonderful gesture'.

An FA Cup Final five days before a European Cup semi-final tie is certainly not the best of preparations, and when the Football Association stake a claim on arguably your best and most influential player, with a plane crash having already robbed you of the majority of the squad that had steered you through to such a prestigious fixture in the first place, then you begin to think that everything is against you and even luck will not see you through. Such was the position that Manchester United found themselves in on Thursday 8 May 1958, when AC Milan flew into Manchester's Ringway Airport with a place in the Final of the European Cup awaiting the winners.

The Football Association's demand for the services of Bobby Charlton was the hardest burden to bear, as it was for little more than a couple of friendly fixtures, the first one being against Portugal at Wembley on 7 May, the eve of Milan's visit to Old Trafford, and then against Yugoslavia in Belgrade on the following Sunday. Rather ironically, he was left out of a third friendly, against Russia on 18 May.

It was back in September that the European campaign had begun in the preliminary round, which had been something of an insult really, having reached the semi-finals during the last season, with the draw pairing them with Irish side Shamrock Rovers. Having seen off the likes of Anderlecht and Bilbao the previous time, the Irish part-timers were certainly not going to cause any real problems, and United ran up a 6–0 scoreline over the water. In a much more closely fought encounter at Old Trafford Shamrock managed to score twice, although United managed three, going through 9–2 on aggregate.

Round one brought another illustrious name from European football, Czechoslovakian side Dukla Prague, but they were no match for Matt Busby's side, returning home after the first leg at Old Trafford having conceded three goals without reply, leaving them with a difficult job in the return match. Three goals were just too much to pull back, and although they did managed to reduce the leeway by one, the United defence stood firm.

In the quarter-finals it was the experienced Red Star Belgrade who stood between United and a second consecutive semi-final place, with the first leg scheduled for Old Trafford. Had the draw been the other way round, who knows what the future would have held.

Under the Old Trafford lights, United, playing in their all-white change strip, managed to gain some form of advantage, winning by the odd goal in three, but they realised that they had something of a mountain to climb in the second leg. Played out on a muddy, slush-covered pitch, United showed why they were beginning to be thought of as one of the best teams in Europe.

Not only did United have to master their opponents and the difficult conditions, but they found another opponent in referee Karl Kajner, whose somewhat poor decisions almost saw United forced into a reply. Two of the Red Star goals came from poor decisions, and back in the dressing room the United players admitted that they were beginning to fear make any form of physical contact with their opponents.

Despite the conditions underfoot United were three goals in front by the interval, with the semi-finals clearly in their sights, but, with the help of the over-officious referee, Red Star pulled it back to 3–3. Had Cokic taken his time when well positioned to score, a third game would have been required to decide the winner.

The events that followed this game have been written about a thousand times and need no repeating here, but despite United's vast problems the show had to go on. Although, on paper at least, Milan were more experienced and certainly better equipped, it was only 90 minutes of football and anything could happen.

There had been much debate as to whether United would actually continue their involvement in the European Cup or withdraw, but the club issued a statement saying, 'We have not at any stage suggested that we would withdraw from the European Cup,' but they did seek a postponement of their first-leg tie against Milan because it was felt that they could not play the semi-final ties on the provisional dates due to their heavy domestic programme. Much to their relief, the Organising Committee agreed to a change of date and Milan travelled to Manchester on Thursday 8 May for the first leg.

The emotions of Munich had carried Jimmy Murphy's roughly assembled side through the FA Cup and into the Final, but Europe was a completely different scenario, although with the voracious Old Trafford crowd behind them anything was possible.

As the game got under way it looked as though it would take more than emotion, luck and the backing of their own supporters to carry United through to the semi-final, as Milan showed their pedigree, with Cucchiaroni and Bredesen causing numerous problems. Defeat looked more than a possibility.

Unsurprisingly, it was the visitors who took the lead in the 24th minute. It was only the courage and strong tackling of the United defence, sometimes bordering between fair and foul, that had kept them on level pegging up until that point. Having broken down yet another Milan attack, Crowther's intended pass to Greaves was intercepted by Bredesen, and before any United player could react to the danger the ball had found its way to Schiaffino, who steered it past Gregg with ease.

Although they continued to dominate, Milan found themselves back on level terms five minutes prior to the interval. Maldini mistimed a pass back to his 'keeper and in stepped Dennis Viollet to seize upon the half-chance.

A challenge between goalscorer Schiaffino and Harry Gregg resulted in the Italian centre-forward receiving a cut on his head, with the injury curtailing his effectiveness in the second

157

Dennis Viollet scored one and won the
penalty in United's 2–1 win over AC Milan.

half of the game, forty-five minutes that saw something of the United of the past few weeks, no doubt inspired by a rousing half-time team talk from Jimmy Murphy.

Galvanised by the diminutive major that was Ernie Taylor, United proceeded to bombard the Italian goal, with Buffon forced into making excellent saves to keep efforts from Goodwin and Taylor out. Webster fired over when he possibly should have done better.

It was by now a typical Cup tie, with both sets of players giving their all and the crowd on their toes or the edge of their seats, kicking every ball in earnest and urging on their favourites in the hope that they could snatch a second goal and ensure victory.

From end to end the ball flew, but still that much-hoped-for breakthrough would not materialise. The minutes were now slowly decreasing, and with only 11 remaining Dennis Viollet set off down the right, beginning yet another assault on the Milan goal. This time, however, instead of looking for a fellow teammate, he decided to go it alone, and after beating a defender he cut inside and headed for goal.

Centre-half Maldini, sensing the danger, moved in for the tackle but Viollet stood his ground, and as the two players moved into the Milan penalty box shoulder to shoulder, a nudge from the tall Italian saw the United number 10 go sprawling on the Old Trafford turf.

Immediately referee Helge from Denmark pointed to the spot, much to the surprise and disgust of Maldini, who threw himself to the ground in anguish as his protesting teammates surrounded the referee to voice their disdain at the decision.

Standing well back from the melee was Ernie Taylor, ball in hand, patiently waiting for all around him to be restored to some form of normality. Eventually the Italians were dispatched to behind the 18-yard line and Taylor coolly placed the ball on the spot. Despite his calmness in the face of the explosive situation, Taylor had decided as he had waited for some sort of order to be restored around him that now was not a time for the finesse side of penalty taking. Instead, he stepped forward and hammered the ball high into the roof of the net, hitting the underside of the cross-bar in the process, almost uprooting the whole structure. As the net bulged the Old Trafford crowd went wild, sensing yet another miraculous victory in the wake of the fateful events of Munich.

Somehow United managed to hold on to their solitary-goal advantage, and despite the Italians feeling more than a little disgruntled at having conceded what they considered to be a rather dubious penalty award when an indirect free-kick would have been more acceptable, they sportingly accepted the handshakes of the United players at the end.

Due to this first-leg match being delayed, the United players knew that if they managed to maintain their advantage in the second leg then they would come face to face with Real Madrid in the Final, giving them the opportunity of extracting revenge for their semi-final defeat the previous season. This, however, would turn out to be little more than a dream, as the journey to Milan saw United not only travel weary but over-powered by the £100,000-valued Italian champions.

The travelling United party had reported to Old Trafford at 1pm on Saturday 10 May, four days before the game, and set off for London by train, where they spent the night. On the Sunday morning they sailed to Calais via Dover and then continued to Milan by train, arriving in the Italian city at 8.20am on Monday 12 May. The journey back was also a prolonged affair, leaving Italy on the Thursday afternoon and arriving back in Manchester on the Saturday evening at 9.40pm.

As for the match, Terence Elliot of the *Daily Express* wrote that it was 'the dirtiest and most foul-studded game it has been my misfortune to see'. Milan got off to the best possible start, opening the scoring as early as the second minute through Schiaffino, who hit the ball past Gregg from 12 yards. Six minutes into the second half they went 2–0 in front on the night when Liedholm scored from the penalty spot.

With half an hour remaining one of the strangest events ever to be witnessed during a United match took place. Although the ball was still in play, the referee blew his whistle to stop the game and the players and spectators stood respectfully for a minute's silence in memory of an Italian FA official.

If this unsettled the United players it made no real difference because the game was by now well out of their reach, and no matter how they had overcome adversity in the past couple of months, their march to the European Cup Final had come to an end. Hopes of revenge against Real Madrid would have to wait.

The Italians added a third in the 70th minute from the foot of Danova, with a fourth coming 10 minutes from time when Schiaffino claimed his second of the night.

United would have to wait a few more years before they could claim both success in Europe and indeed entry into this elite competition, despite being invited to take part in the competition the following year. Once again the stiff-collared members of the English game's governing body stood in United's way. Off the field of play, United had little chance of success.

Manchester United: Gregg, Foulkes, Greaves, Goodwin, Cope, Crowther, Morgans, Taylor, Webster, Viollet, Pearson.
Scorers: Viollet, Taylor.
AC Milan: Buffon, Fontana, Beraldo, Bergamaschi, Maldini, Radice, Mariani, Bredesen, Schiaffino, Leidholm, Cucchiaroni.
Scorer: Schiaffino.
Attendance: 44,880.

No. 26

NORWICH CITY V UNITED

10 January 1959

The haunting memories of Munich were never far away for those associated with United, and many supporters still had visions of the 'Babes' when they watched their beloved red shirts during the course of a game. But with the first anniversary of the crash only a few weeks away, those memories became clearer as the likes of Eddie Colman's hypnotic body swerve and big Dunc's boyish enthusiasm and brute force were fondly remembered.

Having had some element of luck, while at the same time fighting through mentally and physically exhausting games thanks to willpower, inner-strength and the backing of a voracious, enthusiastic support, it was thought, even by the staunchest United supporters, that the following season would see the team begin something of a transitional period, with performances covering a variety of highs and lows as the club got back to some form of normality. But, just like the more modern era, you can never underestimate Manchester United, and they kicked off the 1958–59 season with an excellent 5–2 victory over Chelsea. Munich survivor Bobby Charlton notched a hat-trick and the powerhouse centre-forward Alex Dawson netted the others.

Manchester United 1958–59. Back row, left to right: A. Scanlon, F. Goodwin, H. Gregg, I. Greaves, R. Cope. Front row: E. Taylor, A. Quixall, B. Charlton, W. Foulkes, D. Viollet, W. McGuiness.

NORWICH CITY
FOOTBALL CLUB

F.A. CUP (3rd Round Proper)

SATURDAY, 10th JANUARY, 1959

Norwich City v. Manchester United

PRICE 6d. EACH

It was certainly no fluke as four days later the team scored three at Forest without reply. However, the following game saw them suffer a minor hiccup on the Lancashire Riviera, losing 2–1 at Blackpool, and they subsequently dropped a point at Forest with a 1–1 draw. They did regain their momentum a few miles up the road at Blackburn with a rousing 6–1 victory, Charlton notching his second double of the season, the first having come in the 3–0 win in the first match against Forest; yet there were other defeats, 4–0 against Wolves and 2–0 against Preston

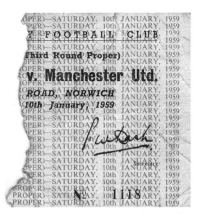

North End in the space of four October days, and an embarrassing 6–3 reversal at nearby Bolton, who were something of a bogey team at the best of times, in mid-November.

Having reached the FA Cup Final in 1957 and 1958, suffering defeats on both occasions, there was an air of determination around the club when January came around with the possibility of the third round kick-starting yet another assault on the twin towers. There were hopes that it would prove to be a case of third time lucky.

When the draw was made, pairing United with Norwich City, there was not any great cause for concern because the Carrow Road side were nothing more than a run-of-the-mill Third Division side, and, in all honesty, not a very successful one at that. They had won eight, drawn eight and lost nine of their 25 games prior to the Cup tie, losing 39 goals – as many as they had scored.

Norwich, due to their Third Division status, had to enter the competition at round one, where they defeated Ilford 3–1 and earned the right to face United by defeating Swindon Town 1–0 in round two. It was a rather confident United who headed to Norwich although at the same time they were well aware of the pitfalls to be found in Cup football and the banana skins that they had slipped on in the not too distant past. Bristol Rovers and Hull City instantly sprung to mind, along with the narrow escapes against Reading, Walthamstow and Hartlepools.

Norwich had enjoyed the best possible Cup preparations with an emphatic 4–0 victory over Southend United the previous Saturday, a performance that was considered their best of the season. Their visitors were also finely tuned following a 3–1 revenge victory over Blackpool at Old Trafford, with Bobby Charlton making it 19 goals for the season after he put two in the back of the net.

Weather conditions were far from ideal as the Carrow Road pitch lay under a two-inch blanket of snow, forcing the referee, Mr W. Clements of West Bromwich, to carry out a pitch inspection at 9.30am. As workmen cleared the touchline and marked it out in blue, the referee carefully considered the overall state of the pitch, deciding that it was playable even though it was a little on the hard side. The weather also affected the special trains carrying most of the 3,000 United support. They still had not reached the ground when the referee's whistle signalled the start of the game, leaving large gaps on the terracing and stand.

All three 'soccer specials' that left Manchester Central Station arrived late. One was 92 minutes late, while the others were over 70 minutes late. The main cause of the problem was the failure of two of the trains to obtain water during the journey south, while the third experienced engine failure. Upon arrival, the starving supporters made a dash for taxis, or those without the necessary cash or who felt fit enough ran to the ground, most arriving 20 minutes into the game.

As the game got under way it soon became obvious that the players were going to find it difficult to maintain their balance and control the ball, and in the early exchanges the home defence were equal to anything that United sent their way, while their attack switched positions in an effort to confuse the United back line.

With four minutes gone the playing conditions came to Norwich's aid as Viollet cut inside from the right and pulled the ball back towards Charlton. The normally reliable marksman failed to keep his balance as his feet slipped in the snow, and the opportunity was gone as the ball ran clear.

Due to the adverse conditions this was no thrill-a-minute Cup tie. Play was much slower than normal, with caution being the name of the game for both teams. Rather than try to pass the ball and make progress up-field, Quixall attempted a long-range effort, but the ball was stopped easily by Nethercott. Norwich were also quick in the use of the long ball, hoping that the United defence would either mis-kick or slip and create a scoring opportunity for one of their forwards.

With 15 minutes gone United were certainly the better side, with Cope and Carolan holding the defence well and coping with the Norwich long balls into the area. In the middle of the field, where most the play was taking place, United were also far superior in their control and ball play. Five minutes later they were shouting for a penalty when Viollet went tumbling into the snow-covered turf. The referee, however, failed to agree.

Not for the first time, something of a melee developed in the Norwich goalmouth as the ball bobbed around two yards from the line. Much to the relief of the home support, Quixall, Viollet and Bradley all had efforts blocked in quick succession. Luck was certainly with the home side.

Having enjoyed most of the play, United were suddenly hit with the unexpected in the 32nd minute. Attacking down the left, Allcock pushed the ball towards Brennan, who then managed to get it into the United area, where Bly was well positioned to slam it into the net from point-blank range.

Inspired by the goal, Norwich, with Allcock commanding in midfield, threw everything they had at United, moving the ball constructively from wing to wing and causing their visitors all sorts of problems. But United refused to panic and, having already done well to keep out an awkward bouncing shot from Hill, Gregg saved again when he stopped a header from the same Norwich player.

Luck certainly wasn't on United's side. With the interval beckoning, a quick move between Viollet and Scanlon caught out the Norwich defence, but between them Nethercott and Butler managed to turn the ball away for a corner.

Refreshed from their half-time break, Norwich once again grabbed the initiative as the second half got under way, and they were unlucky not to score a second goal in the opening minute. Hill centred from the left and up rose Bly to head towards goal, but despite having power behind it, the ball smacked against the crossbar with Gregg beaten, and it bounced to safety.

Hitting the ball first time and hoping for the luck of the bounce, Norwich had the bit between their teeth and, as the ball flew over the heads of the United defenders, they continued to struggle and at times were forced into making errors on the slush-coated pitch. Having the advantage, Norwich were keen to hold onto it and were not duly concerned as to where the ball went as long as it was far away from their goal.

United were again relieved to see the ball miss its intended target in the 52nd minute. McGuinness conceded a free-kick, receiving a severe reprimand from the referee, and the ball was once again lofted towards the visitors' goal and the head of Terry Bly. Yet again he out-jumped Cope and beat Gregg, but Allcock's overhead kick went over the bar. Another long ball down the middle forced Gregg into action again, diving amid a goalmouth scramble to punch the ball out.

Slowly, United began to claw themselves back into the game. Viollet missed the ball completely as he attempted to volley home a Scanlon cross, but Norwich stuck manfully to the task at hand and were always quick to cause problems for Harry Gregg and his fellow defenders, with the United goalkeeper fortunate not to be picking the ball out of his net in the 57th minute. With Bly prompting the attack, Brennan's shot hit the foot of the post, and from the re-bound Hill could only watch as his goal-bound effort hit Foulkes.

Play swung rapidly from end to end as the conditions under foot continued to deteriorate, but as some began to sense that United might snatch an equaliser, their hopes were crushed by a second Norwich goal in the 65th minute. Again Bly broke away, this time on the left, and Gregg did well to stop his shot, but the ball only broke to the feet of Crossan. Hitting a rather weak shot towards goal, Gregg scrambled back and grasped the ball without much of a problem. Rather surprisingly, however, the referee signalled that the ball had crossed the line and awarded a goal.

On the hour mark Bly forced his way forward once again but was foiled by Gregg, while minutes later at the opposite end Charlton, the main hope for any United revival, was blatantly fouled as he moved forward. The free-kick, however, came to nothing. Quixall saw a shot fly narrowly past the post, then Scanlon forced a superb full-length save out of Nethercott with a tremendous drive as United fought to rescue something from the game.

Bly really should have put the game beyond doubt with 15 minutes remaining, but he misjudged Crossan's centre and the ball went wide of Gregg's goal. But the Norwich centre-forward made no mistake two minutes from time when he crowned a superb and memorable victory for the Canaries with an excellent solo effort.

Obtaining the ball on the left, Bly brushed past Ronnie Cope as the centre-half slithered in the slush, and he avoided another half-hearted challenge before shooting past Gregg from a narrow angle.

There was certainly no way back for United now, and as the final whistle blew, thousands of delighted Norwich fans invaded the pitch to salute their heroes. Their United counterparts slunk slowly away into the dark East Anglian evening, heading back to their train for the long journey back to the North West.

In the brief *Manchester Evening News* front-page summary, the stay-at-home supporters read, 'There is no excuse for the Reds. Humble Third Division Norwich beat them fair and square. United never mastered the conditions. But don't blame the snow. They just weren't good enough, folks.'

Busby, as ever, was gracious in defeat, telling his opposite number Archie Macaulay, 'You beat us by playing football. Norwich played the correct game, whereas we did not change our tactics to suit the conditions.'

In a way, United were unfortunate, as on another day, they would most probably have taken three or four goals off Norwich. Had the game been scheduled for the following week, there would have been a good chance of it being postponed due to the weather, and had it been so, the players might have been in a better frame of mind or the conditions at Carrow Road much better.

There were no excuses. United were poor on the day and did not deserve anything from the game, whereas Norwich, comfortable on their own ground, took the game to United and reaped the benefits.

The result was certainly a shock to the system, but seven days later United found their scoring boots again, beating Swansea Town 6–4 in a friendly, while Norwich were in the process of progressing into round five of the FA Cup with a 3–2 home win over Cardiff City. In United's first League fixture following the Cup exit, they scored four, although they also conceded four at home to Newcastle, but at least the show was back on the road.

As for Norwich, round five took them to Tottenham, where they earned a creditable 1–1 draw, winning the replay 1–0. The quarter-finals saw them paired with Sheffield United, and again they were certainly up for the Cup, holding the Blades to a 1–1 draw. Carrow Road claimed yet another victim in the replay, which Norwich won 3–2, taking them into the semi-finals. This was only the third time a Third Division side had reached this stage of the competition.

Drawn against Luton Town, with the tie to be played at the already familiar White Hart Lane, Norwich had an excellent opportunity to go all the way to Wembley. Despite finding themselves a goal behind at half-time they managed an equaliser, but the replay at Birmingham City's St Andrew's was where their luck unfortunately ran out, and they lost 1–0.

Manchester United: Gregg, Foulkes, Carolan, Goodwin, Cope, McGuinness, Bradley, Quixall, Charlton, Viollet, Scanlon.
Norwich City: Nethercott, Thurlow, Ashman, McCrohan, Butler, Crowe, Crossan, Allcock, Bly, Hill Brennan.
Scorers: Bly 2, Crossan.
Attendance: 38,000.

No. 27

UNITED V NEWCASTLE UNITED
31 January 1959

It is not often that Manchester United score four goals at Old Trafford and fail to win, especially when they had been leading 4–1 at half-time, but the visit of Newcastle United on the last day of January 1959 was one of those days. The 90 minutes certainly produced value for money, but the Old Trafford faithful made their way out of the stadium shaking their heads and wondering how such a lead was squandered.

United had gone into the game on the back of a run of eight consecutive League victories, although the previously mentioned FA Cup defeat at Norwich was an unforeseen and entirely unexpected blip on what had been a favourable season to date. The visit of Newcastle United to Manchester saw the return of former fans' favourite, Charlie Mitten, now manager of the Geordies, and although his side were not in a challenging position for the Championship they were comfortably placed in mid-table and were one of the top scoring sides in the division.

Earlier in the week the Old Trafford pitch had been under hard frost, but by the time the match kicked-off a thaw had made conditions rather soft, and although some parts of the ground were slippery underfoot the players soon adapted, with the Newcastle forwards quickly switching positions and causing the United defence some early problems.

United, however, soon gained the upper hand and, following one corner, which was scrambled away, a number of shots were sent in the direction of the visitors' goal, all of which were blocked. But such was the pressure exerted upon the visitors it was only a matter of time before the opening goal materialised, and with the game only five minutes old, United were in front. Quixall had already forced goalkeeper Harvey into making a fine save before Scanlon scurried down the wing, skipped past full-back Keith and then cut inside, heading for goal. As the winger neared the goal, Keith had made up the lost ground and was suddenly behind him and rather clumsily brought him crashing to the ground. Without a moment's hesitation the referee pointed to the spot. Up stepped Bobby Charlton, and his kick smacked against the underside of the Newcastle crossbar and into the net to put United in front.

Newcastle quickly tried to create an equaliser, with Scoular's long forward passes setting up numerous attacks, and from one such pass Gregg only just managed to fist away McGuigan's curling centre before White could get his head to it. In the 23rd minute, they missed an even better opportunity to draw level when their right-winger, Taylor, sent a perfect centre towards the United goal, but Allchurch completely missed the ball from point-

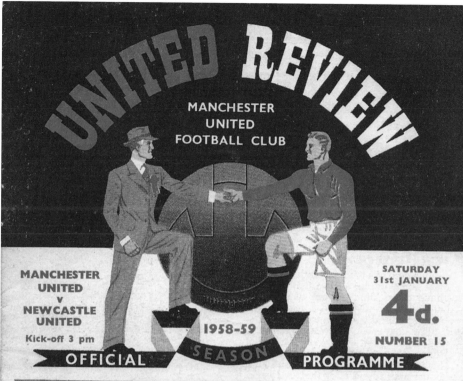

MANCHESTER
UNITED
FOOTBALL CLUB

UNITED REVIEW

MANCHESTER
UNITED
V
NEWCASTLE
UNITED
Kick-off 3 pm

OFFICIAL

1958-59
SEASON

SATURDAY
31st JANUARY

4d.

NUMBER 15

PROGRAMME

TEAMWORK AT OLD TRAFFORD!

Just in case you ever wondered what footballers did when they weren't playing football (our last league match was on 3rd January) our photo provides the answer! Dennis Viollet is typically hardworking and Bill Foulkes appears fully in command of the situation. Fred Goodwin is on the wing whilst Bobby Charlton schemes his next move.

This photograph was taken by the Manchester Evening News to whom we are glad to make acknowledgement

blank range. The ball continued across goal and was collected by White, but once again Gregg came to United's rescue by flinging his body across his goal to block the shot.

Despite Newcastle's determination, which had seen Taylor hit the side netting and Foulkes deflect the ball wide for a corner, it was United who found the net, with Quixall scoring their second in the 27th minute. Scanlon was again the supplier, pushing the ball through to the big-money signing, who was standing just outside the penalty area in what the Newcastle defenders thought to be an offside position, but as no whistle materialised Quixall took the ball forward, rounded goalkeeper Harvey and pushed the ball into the vacant net.

The visitors once again rallied and on this occasion did manage to pull a goal back three minutes later. Attacking down the middle, Allchurch, from the edge of the penalty area, caught a brief glimpse of goal through a mass of bodies and past the outstretched arm of Harry Gregg.

Newcastle's resurgence was short lived, though, as they were suddenly swept aside, and not only did United increase their lead, but they were 4–1 in front with two goals in as many minutes.

First it was Albert Scanlon, celebrating his call up to the England Under-23 squad in style, who had drifted inside, taking up the centre-forward role, fastening onto a lob forward from Quixall. The winger moved forward on goal and, despite the close attentions of Scott, hit the ball firmly past Harvey.

Sixty seconds later it was Viollet who added the fourth, following good work from Bradley, who beat three men, the third by strength rather than skill, before working the ball over to Viollet.

Charlton almost made it five, but Harvey managed to push the ball round the post to safety, then Viollet found himself only a couple of yards from goal with the ball at his feet, but his shot was blocked and kicked to safety.

As the interval approached, United continued to press, although Newcastle did manage the odd attack and certainly looked dangerous, despite being three goals behind. No sooner had the second half got under way than the visitors were on the attack, revitalised by a mixture of their half-time refreshments and Charlie Mitten's pep talk. Allchurch managed to break through the United defence, but his shot was saved by Gregg.

Eastham, like Allchurch, was coming more and more into the game and had a shot deflected wide by Foulkes as the visitors began to enjoy most of the play. Such persistence was finally rewarded in the 69th minute when White headed an excellent centre from an Allchurch cross. A minute later there was only one goal separating the two sides as White once again got the better of the United defence, scoring from 12 yards out.

United now had their backs to the wall, having earlier in the game enjoyed the bulk of the play, and Goodwin, Carolan and Foulkes were severely tested, although Newcastle struggled to find a way through. But as the game moved into the final quarter of an hour, United were to find themselves even more stretched as Newcastle piled on the pressure, with Jimmy Scoular, who had repelled the United players in a fashion that would have gained five stars from King Canute, feeding his forwards with a constant supply of passes, which saw the home defence finally crack in the 76th minute when his free-kick found McGuigan, standing unmarked, who drove the ball left-footed into the bottom corner of Gregg's goal, setting up something of an all-action finale in the process. Supporters who usually left the ground prior to full-time were now rather loath to do so in case they missed something in what had turned into a pulsating encounter.

Forcing a couple of corners, United came closest to snatching a winner, while Keith also managed to scramble a Bradley shot off the line, but, despite the pressure, the honours were shared.

Prior to kick-off, this fixture could easily have been billed as nothing more than an ordinary, run-of-the-mill 90 minutes, but having sat through the action-packed game in the Old Trafford press box, Eric Todd of the *Manchester Guardian* wrote, 'In speculating on the proceedings a few hours previously, one suggested there would be no lack of entertainment: events proved this to be one of the major understatements of the season. Rarely is the average football supporter privileged to see such simultaneous artistry from four inside-forwards – a theatre-goer might experience the same uplift by watching Olivier, Wolfitt, Redgrave, and Richardson in the same play – and even less frequently is there such a remarkable regression in the tide of events.'

It certainly wasn't the first occasion that Newcastle had travelled south to Manchester, found themselves three goals behind and salvaged something from the game, as they had travelled to Maine Road two years previously and had been 3–0 down, only to come back and win 5–4 in extra-time. This, however, was United, but all credit had to be given to the visitors for their retaliatory power, and where the home side enjoyed the best of the first 45 minutes it was the visitors who could claim the second 45.

For United it was certainly a point dropped, the third post-war occasion that they had scored four and failed to win. The other three games, against Aston Villa in 1955–56, Liverpool in 1953–54 and Huddersfield Town in 1947–48, all finished in 4–4 draws. If you venture back to season 1936–37, however, United scored four against Derby County on 5 September and actually lost 5–4.

The point, thrown away, kept United in fourth place in the First Division, three points behind leaders Arsenal with a game in hand. Three weeks later, following victories over Tottenham away (3–1), City at home (4–1) and current League leaders Wolves at home (2–1), they were in second place, but the Midlands side just could not be dislodged from that top spot and were eventually crowned champions.

It was a valiant and certainly creditable achievement, and one that no one could have envisaged back in August. The problem now was to maintain that level of performance and build on it in the future.

Manchester United: Gregg, Foulkes, Carolan, Harrop, Goodwin, McGuinness, Bradley, Quixall, Viollet, Charlton, Scanlon.
Scorers: Charlton, Scanlon, Quixall, Viollet.
Newcastle United: Harvey, Keith, McMichael, Scoular, Scott, Franks, Taylor, Allchurch, White, Eastham, McGuigan.
Scorers: White 2, Allchurch, McGuigan.
Attendance: 48,777.

UNITED V WOLVERHAMPTON WANDERERS
21 February 1959

There was a huge sigh of relief around Old Trafford, and indeed the whole of Manchester, when season 1957–58 finally came to an end underneath Wembley Stadium's twin towers. It had been a season that had promised so much. But despite the tears, it had ended with heads held high; despite the memories that would linger on for eternity, there was hope for the future and a new beginning for Manchester United.

In the aftermath of the disaster at Munich, no one, not even the most fanatical supporter, could have envisaged the gut-wrenching performances that were churned out by the makeshift Red Devils, striding powerfully to Wembley Stadium while coping admirably with the physically and mentally draining rigours of the First Division.

A third consecutive title had been more than a possibility mid-way through season 1957–58, but in the end, they had to be happy with ninth place. Wolverhampton Wanderers claimed the crown, some 21 points better off than United. There were defeats, as was expected, including four consecutive ones in the League fixtures of March, but there were no tantrums, no talks of a crisis, as each game was something of a learning curve on the long road back to footballing normality around Manchester.

Following a summer of recharging the batteries, as well as the regaining of fitness for some, August once again appeared on the calendars, signalling the start of yet another domestic football season and one that would be as vital as any in the history of Matt Busby and his team. Wolves would certainly be there or thereabouts in 1958–59, but what of United?

There should actually have been three competitions for United to enter in 1958–59, but due to red tape they found themselves banned from taking part in one of those. The organisers of the European Cup had invited United to take part in the 1958–59 competition as a 'gesture of sympathy' after the events of the previous year; however, with the opening round of the prestigious tournament only weeks away, United were informed by the Football Association Consultative Committee that because United were not 'champions', they did not qualify to take part. United issued a statement following their weekly board meeting four days after receiving the verdict and said the following:

> 'The FA in their letter of July 5th stated that they had no objection to Manchester United entering the European Cup this season.

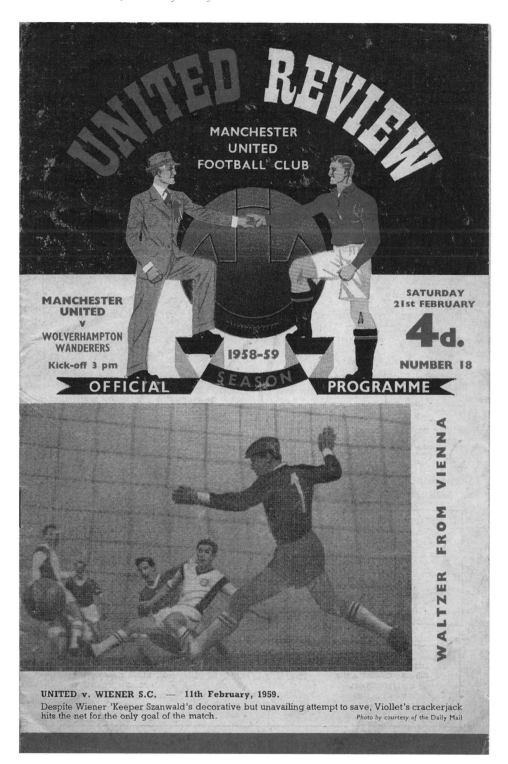

UNITED v. WIENER S.C. — 11th February, 1959.
Despite Wiener 'Keeper Szanwald's decorative but unavailing attempt to save, Viollet's crackerjack hits the net for the only goal of the match. *Photo by courtesy of the Daily Mail*

'The Football League wrote to the club that they could not give their consent to the club to enter. The club appealed to the League's Board of Appeal, and this appeal was upheld.

'The decision of the Board of Appeal is, by the rules of the Football League, FINAL.

'Therefore, the club were allowed by the FA to enter the competition. By the decision of the Board of Appeal, which is FINAL, the Football League were prevented from interfering with our entry.

'In these circumstances there was no reason why the dates we submitted to the Football Association should not be approved, nor why the FA should depart from the terms of their letter of July 5th in which they stated as before mentioned "The Football Association has no objection to you taking part."'

Thus, it was just the FA Cup and the First Division that Manchester United would be in contention for, and because of the above decision, Matt Busby's team were even more determined that ever to be one of the teams in the hat for the 1959–60 European Cup, not as gatecrashers but as champions.

Opening the campaign with a home fixture against Chelsea, the Londoners were taken as much by surprise as anyone, as United brushed their opponents aside with a 5–2 victory. Munich survivor Bobby Charlton notched up a hat-trick, with one of the success stories of the previous campaign, Alex Dawson, claiming the other two. Charlton, the scars now purely mental, seemed to take on the mantle of the on-field leader, although without the captaincy, scoring eight in the opening five games. United lost only two of their opening 10 fixtures, with the five goals against Chelsea surpassed with six against Blackburn Rovers.

Many, however, thought that the bubble had burst in October, with consecutive defeats against Wolves away (4–0), and Preston North End at home (2–0). Although they managed a 1–1 draw against Arsenal at Old Trafford, they stumbled to a further two defeats against Everton, 3–2 away, and West Bromwich Albion, 2–1 at home.

November was slightly better, the team winning three out of the five fixtures, although the 6–3 defeat at Bolton did little to help the morale. But this was nothing more than a slight dip in form, which had been expected, and as the year moved into its final four weeks the momentum was once again picked up, with Birmingham City on the last Saturday in November, Leicester City and Preston North End all conceding four. Chelsea failed to gain revenge at Stamford Bridge for their five-goal hammering and let in another three, while Aston Villa were beaten twice on consecutive days over the Christmas period.

Such results lifted United from 14th, following the 2–1 reversal at the Hawthorns on 25 October, to fourth on 27 December after Mark Pearson and Dennis Viollet's goals had given them a 2–0 win at Villa Park. Wolves still led the way with 32 points from their 24 games, but United were now a mere three points behind, although they had played one game more.

The results going into the New Year continued to be favourable, at least in the League, with the 'goals for' column on the table taking on a more healthy appearance on a weekly basis.

Wolves, having momentarily lost the top spot to Arsenal, were again leading the field as what was going to be perhaps the crunch game of the season drew near.

On the morning of Saturday 21 February Wolverhampton Wanderers travelled north to Manchester, sitting on top of the First Division with 38 points from their 28 games, having defeated Leeds United 6–2 the previous Saturday. Seven days earlier United had pushed neighbours City nearer to the foot of the table with a 4–1 defeat. They were now in third place, level on points with Arsenal. Only their 'goals against' column let them down. It was champions versus contenders, with the winner, although not a certainty for the title, at least gaining some advantage as the season progressed.

Old Trafford was obviously packed, with a number of turnstiles closed well before kick-off. The falling drizzle blowing down the pitch and into the faces of those packing the open scoreboard end did little to keep the supporters of both teams away.

The visitors, although kicking-off, almost immediately lost possession, and Scanlon threatened down the left, beating Stuart with ease. His low centre across the sodden, muddy pitch was completely missed by a Wolves defender directly in front of goal, but there was no one there to take advantage. A similar incident occurred moments later from a Viollet cross, but on this occasion the ball swerved away from the waiting red shirts, allowing Wright to clear.

Such was the pressure that Wolves were under in those opening stages that Stuart brought down Bradley, putting his team under unnecessary pressure, then the Wolves right-back was tormented by Scanlon, with one of the United outside-left's crosses finding Quixall, whose shot was tipped over by Finlayson. Play was almost constantly in the Wolves' half of the pitch, and all that Gregg had to deal with was a simple pass back.

Goodwin, well in command in the middle, sent Scanlon scurrying away down the left. Stuart was once again left floundering but was grateful to see the ball bobble in front of Quixall as he prepared to shoot, and the United man fired over the bar.

Gregg punched clear a header from Deeley in the 20th minute, while three minutes later Charlton missed a golden opportunity to put United in front. McGuinness got the ball out to Quixall, who threaded the ball through the middle to Charlton as he broke clear. With only Finlayson to beat, the usually dependable goal machine shot wide.

Slowly, the visitors began to get into the game. Deeley was too slow to react to a short corner, then Broadbent, although getting the better of Greaves, failed to test Gregg. But it was still United who enjoyed most of the play, and from a Scanlon corner Charlton's solid header was cleared off the line by Harris.

Viollet also had the opportunity to score the opening goal, with Charlton on this occasion the provider, but having dribbled round Finlayson, the ball ran out of play. This was rather unusual for Viollet, taking the whole 90 minutes into consideration, as the United centre-forward was in excellent form, giving England captain and Wolves centre-half Billy Wright a torturous afternoon.

With five minutes remaining to half-time, United finally got the goal that they had been threatening to score. Charlton's centre was headed out by Flowers but only as far as Viollet, who caught it on the half-volley, driving the ball through the packed goalmouth and in off the post.

Harry Gregg.

Not only was it an important time to score, it also came when Wolves were beginning to threaten, resorting to long passes in order to try and get the better of the United defence because little else seemed to have much of an impact.

Just before the interval Bradley chased the ball into the Wolves' area and put Finlayson under enough pressure to see the 'keeper drop the ball. Fortunately for the visitors, it was scrambled clear. Scanlon attempted a similar move soon afterwards but found himself penalised by the referee for raising his foot. Both incidents seemed to unsettle Wolves, and Clamp was spoken to for a foul on Scanlon, but only after the United player had extracted revenge with a tackle from behind on the Wolves player.

After the interval, as the rain continued to fall, Wolves attempted to get at least back on level terms, but the United defence stood firm, with Harry Gregg showing why he had been voted the best goalkeeper in the 1958 World Cup, throwing himself at one cross from Deeley and knocking out Murray in the process.

As the second half progressed, the game was delicately balanced, with United always threatening to score a second while the visitors continued to stretch the home defence to its limits. Gregg was fortunate on one occasion when he lost possession while saving from Murray, and Greaves had to step in to kick clear.

With 64 minutes gone Wolves finally broke the United defence and equalised. Mason grabbed possession in midfield and charged forward, passing two United defenders in the process. From just outside the area he let fly, and his shot bounced on the wet surface in front of the unsighted and wrong-footed Gregg into the net. Even some of the supporters were caught out and at first were uncertain as to what had actually happened.

It was a poor goal to loose, but United were unruffled and fought back. Stuart was again spoken to by the referee after another heavy tackle on Scanlon. Charlton beat Finlayson but could only watch in despair as his shot rebounded off the post and caught him in a position from which he couldn't force the ball over the line at a second attempt.

For 23 of the final 25 minutes both sides continued to miss scoring opportunities. Broadbent twice came close, as did Charlton, with Bradley running up and down the right wing unmarked. But it wasn't until the final minute that the outcome of the game was determined.

Bradley once again took off down the right flank then pushed the ball forward towards Viollet, who immediately cut in towards goal and split the Wolves' defence with a pass to Charlton. On this occasion, he thankfully blasted the ball past Finlayson on the turn from eight yards out, much to the delight of the home supporters in the still-packed stadium as the rain continued to fall. Some, however, had called it a day sometime earlier, convinced the outcome was going to be a draw.

It was, therefore, a valuable two points won, putting United as joint leaders on 38 points, with 12 games remaining (Wolves had 13), but seven days later all that good work was completely and utterly undone.

United travelled to third-place Arsenal, hopeful of building on the victory over Wolves, but within 25 minutes of the kick-off Arsenal were 3–0 in front with the United defence having endured a real hammering. Viollet pulled a goal back, then a Scanlon free-kick hit the post, but the minutes slowly ticked away, and although Bradley notched a second there was only one minute remaining, giving United no chance of salvaging anything from the game.

Another seven days on and the applecart was overturned again, but with League leaders Wolves really gaining the advantage as they hammered Arsenal at Molineux by six goals to one. United got back on track with a 2–1 win over Everton.

By the end of March, there was a point in it, although Wolves still had that valuable game in hand. Then disaster struck for United. They lost 4–2 at Burnley, a result that should more or less have ended their Championship dreams. That was until Wolves drew 3–3 with Burnley, while United beat Bolton 3–0. Seven days later Wolves drew 2–2 with Bolton, but it was a day when the United forward line left their shooting boots back in Manchester as they drew 0–0 with Luton.

The following Saturday it was all over. In spite of United's 1–0 victory over Birmingham City at Old Trafford, Wolves put five past Luton and they certainly could not now be caught. Even if it had gone to the final day, they would still have clinched it as they won 1–0 at Goodison while United lost 2–1 at Leicester.

Despite the disappointment of losing the Championship it was a commendable achievement, finishing runners-up in a season when everyone would have been happy with a mid-table placing.

Taking up the European Cup challenge would just have to wait.

Manchester United: Gregg, Greaves, Carolan, Goodwin, Cope, McGuinness, Bradley, Quixall, Viollet, Charlton, Scanlon.
Scorers: Charlton, Viollet.
Wolverhampton Wanderers: Finlayson, Stuart, Harris, Clamp, Wright, Flowers, Lill, Mason, Murray, Broadbent, Deeley.
Scorer: Mason.
Attendance: 62,794.

No. 29

CHELSEA V UNITED

2 September 1959

Having rather miraculously finished runners-up in the First Division title race of 1958–59, considering the aftermath of Munich, Matt Busby and, perhaps just as importantly, Jimmy Murphy had at least something to build on. Despite that lofty position, however, no one was fooled into thinking that the future was rosy. Most were more than aware that there were difficult times ahead with much rebuilding required, especially at the lower end of the scale, with the youngsters thrown in at the deep end now finding the going tough.

There was no activity on the transfer front in the summer of 1959 and the United management actually began the new campaign with the same 11 that finished the previous season, with the exception of Shay Brennan, who had made his only appearance of 1958–59 in that final fixture at Leicester, coming in to replace Wilf McGuinness, who had missed only two of the other 41 fixtures.

United travelled to the Midlands on the opening day of the 1959–60 season, visiting West Bromwich Albion, but the 3–2 defeat, with the home side fighting back twice to snatch the points, left Matt Busby pondering over whether or not to spend some of the £26,000 profit from the previous season on strengthening his squad.

An injury to Alex Dawson in the following fixture against Chelsea, the first at Old Trafford, saw the burly Scot carried from the field on a stretcher and the 10-man United side lose to a solitary Jimmy Greaves goal. Busby, however, insisted that he was happy with the players that he had, saying, 'We have got to give the lads who finished second in the League last season a fair chance. It is much too early to start worrying. Just because we have lost a couple of early games, there's no need to think the world's come to an end.'

Three days after Chelsea's visit to Old Trafford, United entertained Newcastle United but struggled to beat the bottom-of-the-League side 3–2, with headlines such as 'United Must Plug This Leak' and 'United Defence Is Sluggish' being found among the reports on the game.

Even though the season was still in its infancy, there were many who considered that United had problems and that they should be attended to sooner rather than later. Having failed against Chelsea at Old Trafford, despite being reduced to 10 men, the visit to Stamford Bridge on the first Saturday in September would most probably see the struggle continue, despite the London club not having enjoyed the best of starts themselves. Jimmy Greaves had scored a hat-trick for Chelsea on the opening day against Preston North End as United were held to a 4–4

LEAGUE CHAMPIONS 1954-55

Chelsea
Football Club

Stamford Bridge Grounds, London SW6

FOOTBALL LEAGUE—DIVISION I   SEASON 1959-60

CHELSEA
v
MANCHESTER UNITED

Wednesday, 2nd Sept., 1959   Kick-off 7.30 p.m.

Official Programme 6d.   The right of admission to grounds
is reserved.

draw, and while United were struggling against Newcastle, Chelsea were being hammered 3–1 at Leicester City. But despite their rather indifferent beginning, Chelsea was still expected to overcome United.

Thousands converged on Stamford Bridge for the Wednesday night fixture, catching the South London club somewhat unprepared. With kick-off fast approaching, cars outside the ground were damaged as fans trampled over them in a mad rush to reach the turnstiles. Others, sensing that the chances of gaining admission were remote, attempted to gain admission by scaling the floodlight pylons, using the power cables as a rope, such was their desperation and urgency to see the game.

Inside the ground, many of those who had gained admission struggled to find a suitable vantage point, being pushed and shoved across the spacious terracing, ending up on the cinder track around the side of the pitch. Others found the conditions inside too much, fainting as the crushing increased and the turnstiles continued to click merrily away, with the club officials oblivious to the increasingly dangerous situation arising within the stadium.

Outside the ground a traffic policeman said, 'The whole thing became a shambles.' While inside, many decided that they were never going to see any of the game and decided to leave the ground and ask for their money back, thus causing further problems when the gates were opened to let them out, as 60 policemen struggled to prevent an even greater number gaining access.

Some supporters tried in vain to complain to the Chelsea directors, safely and comfortably seated in the directors' box; others spoke of how they saw those who had fainted being treated and women screaming while at the same time the turnstiles were still open and taking money from supporters who were obviously going to experience a problem once they made their way up the steps onto the terracing.

Those who had managed to escape the crush and get out of the ground made their way round towards the club offices, shouting 'Thieves!' at passing gatemen with their bags full of money. On arrival at the locked up offices, three mounted policemen stood guard as officials refused to see the baying crowd.

Club Secretary John Battersby later said, 'We have had up to 80,000 in here. Thousands are bound not to see if early arrivals don't move forward. It's up to them.' Another official was to add, 'Reports from inside the ground gave no indication that the late arrivals would not get a view of the match, so we did not lock the gates. We have no power to refund the money.'

With 25 minutes gone it looked as though the home side were going to repeat their Old Trafford victory when Jimmy Greaves gave them the lead. Frank Blunstone broke forward, but his shot was blocked by Harry Gregg. However, the ball fell nicely for Greaves to have nothing more to do than tap it home. It was a lead that they held for only 60 seconds though. Albert Scanlon took the ball down the wing towards the Chelsea goal, winning a corner. From the kick, the ball found its way to Albert Quixall, and the former Sheffield Wednesday man managed to squeeze the ball between the Chelsea 'keeper and the post into the net.

Within a matter of minutes United were in front. Warren Bradley weaved his way down the right before crossing the ball, and as the Chelsea defence stood still, Bobby Charlton rose into the night air to nod the ball past Matthews in the Chelsea goal. Bradley made it 3–1 five minutes later, latching onto the end of a Charlton/Viollet move and making goalscoring look simple.

Chelsea pulled one back five minutes prior to the interval when Peter Sillett drove a 30-yard free-kick past a rather statuette Harry Gregg, the United 'keeper having come off his goalline, standing motionless as the ball curved over his head and into the net.

As the players left the field for the half-time interval, conditions outside threatened to get out of hand, and it was finally decided to allow many of those outside into the ground to join fellow supporters around the dog track. How many were allowed admission was obviously unrecorded, making the official attendance of 66,579 completely wrong.

Scanlon, not for the first time, got the better of Sillett a minute after the restart and rolled the ball towards Viollet, who gratefully accepted the opportunity to restore United's two-goal advantage, allowing the visitors to settle down and play the type of football that many had begun to associate Manchester United with.

Bradley was having an inspired game on the right, while Greaves was not enjoying the best of evenings under the watchful eye of the United defence. Charlton was, at times, little more than a blur under the floodlights, with Quixall and Viollet combining superbly in the middle of the field. But it was Warren Bradley, the United outside-right, who was behind the visitors increasing their lead in the 72nd minute, prodding the ball home from close in.

Strangely, Chelsea were allowed back into the game a minute later when Brennan, in the side in place of Goodwin, inexplicably pulled the ball down with his hands while standing on the penalty spot despite not being under any pressure. Sillett claimed his second of the evening when he blasted the ball past Gregg. Could the home side mount something of a fight-back, forcing the sometimes delicate-looking United defence into making further errors?

With 10 minutes remaining the question was answered when Bradley once again thrilled the crowd with some exceptional wing-play before knocking the ball across goal for Viollett to score United's sixth.

'Old Manchester Magic' proclaimed the headlines on the back pages the following day, along with 'Wizard Warren Leads United's 6–3 Saunter' and 'Bradley Dances Through Dazed Chelsea Defence'. The game also made the front pages, with the *Daily Express* splashing 'Money-Back Cry at Manchester United Game – Night Soccer Row' across the top of its Thursday morning edition.

Was this the lift-off that Matt Busby's side needed? Unfortunately not, as they could only manage a draw three days later at Birmingham City, although in the next fixture against Leeds United at Old Trafford they hit the Yorkshire side for six without reply. This was strangely followed by a 5–1 thumping at Tottenham and a 2–2 draw in the return game against Leeds.

The inconsistency continued throughout the season, with the next two fixtures bringing consecutive defeats against City (3–0) and Preston North End (4–0), only to be followed by two victories, thus setting something of a pattern as they could never lift themselves to win three games in succession.

In December they would beat Blackpool 3–1 at Old Trafford and then Nottingham Forest 5–1 away before losing at home 3–2 to West Bromwich Albion and 2–1 to Burnley. Two days later at Turf Moor they won 4–1, but on 2 January a much-improved Newcastle United inflicted a 7–3 hammering in the North East.

February saw them lose 3–1 at Leicester only to bounce back three days later at Blackpool, winning 6–0. March and April told similar stories, the team playing in a 5–0 victory at Fulham then a 4–2 defeat at Sheffield Wednesday. They gained both points in a 5–3 win over West Ham United at Old Trafford then failed in a 5–2 defeat at Highbury before rounding off the season a week later with a 5–0 win over Everton at home. Few would have selected United when contemplating their weekly Football Pools.

Finishing seventh was obviously a disappointment, but it was a clear indication to everyone associated with the club that there was a lot of work to be done. Strangely though, Matt Busby was reluctant to splash the cash until late 1960, when he brought in the midfield power of Maurice Setters from West Bromwich Albion, to be followed slightly less than a year later by defender Noel Cantwell from West Ham United.

Slowly, the backbone of a new Manchester United was taking shape. David Herd finally arrived from Arsenal in the summer of 1961, with Denis Law following the following year. The Scottish trio was completed by the arrival of Pat Crerand, a signing that not only played a significant part in steering the club towards FA Cup success but also was a major part in keeping the club in the First Division. That, however, is another story.

Chelsea: Matthews, Sillett, Whittaker, Anderton, Scott, Compton, Brabrook, Greaves, Livesey, Nicholas, Blunstone.
Scorers: Sillett 2 (1 penalty), Greaves.
Manchester United: Gregg, Cope, Carolan, Brennan, Foulkes, McGuinness, Bradley, Quixall, Viollet, Charlton, Scanlon.
Scorers: Bradley 2, Quixall, Charlton, Viollet.
Attendance: 66,579.

UNITED V REAL MADRID

1 October 1959

Despite the somewhat unsavoury scenes that had blighted United's European Cup semi-final against Real Madrid at Old Trafford back in April 1957, a friendship was forged over the two legs that still lasts today, despite the various transfers and rumours of further departures from Manchester to the sunshine of the Spanish capital.

Following the Munich disaster, the Madrid hierarchy were quick to contact Jimmy Murphy, offering whatever help they could, with even the talk of Puskas making the move from Madrid to Manchester. However, it wasn't until season 1959–60 that the platonic embrace between the two clubs actually blossomed, when fixtures between the two were arranged, but it was to be little more than a learning curve as far as United were concerned, with Real Madrid continuing to rule the roost as far as European football was concerned.

The Spaniards, with the likes of Di Stefano, Gento, Munoz and Rial in their line-up, had lifted the European Cup in its inaugural season of 1955–56, defeating Stade de Reims 4–3 in the Final, played at the Parc de Princes Stadium in Paris, then went on to retain it in 1956–57, 1957–58 and 1958–59. They were now the benchmark for any team wishing to be successful on more than simply their domestic front.

The Madrid side of 1959 could still boast of the incredible talent of Di Stefano and Gento but had not stood still in their quest to be the ultimate footballing side, adding the Hungarian maestro Puskas and the multi-talented Brazilian Didi to the ranks, alongside the home-grown Santamaria. This was a formidable five-a-side team that would have wiped the floor with anyone, even without a goalkeeper. It was with those illustrious names that Real Madrid rolled into Manchester on 1 October 1959 for what was the 'home' leg of a double-header against the best team around.

United, having rallied in the wake of Munich, surprised everyone by finishing runners-up in 1958–59, but the following

MANCHESTER UNITED F. C. LTD.

STAND	ROW	SEAT
C	T	126

Grand Challenge Match

Manchester United v. Real Madrid

AT OLD TRAFFORD   KICK OFF 7-30 p.m.

THURSDAY, 1st OCTOBER, 1959

20/- incl. Tax

NO MONEY RETURNED   *Olive*
           Secretary.

KEEP THIS PORTION

A SPECIAL
EDITION OF
THE OFFICIAL
M.U.F.C.
PROGRAMME

1st OCTOBER, 1959

NUMBER FIVE

Manchester United

VERSUS

Real Madrid

GRAND
CHALLENGE
MATCH

KICK-OFF
7-30 pm

4d.

campaign, 1959–60, was going to be entirely different. The game against the Spanish giants would certainly be an ideal opportunity for manager Matt Busby to gauge how his team were progressing and where it needed strengthening, while it also gave the Manchester public an opportunity to watch the masters at work.

Some 60-odd thousand cast their normal routine to one side and made their way to Old Trafford for the Thursday night fixture, an unusual night for the floodlights down beside the Ship Canal to be shinning brightly. But they provided an ideal backdrop, perhaps more like the footlights of some West End theatre, picking out the visitors in their all-white strip as they traipsed across their temporary stage.

Although billed as a friendly, it certainly wasn't treated as such. An 'exhibition game' might be a more apt description, but the 6–1 defeat makes that particular statement sound as if United were simply there to make up the numbers, playing the stooge to the main attraction. Nothing could be further from the truth.

The headlines of the following day's newspapers were equally blunt. 'A Real Hiding For Busby Boys – Shooting Senors Smack In Six' was splashed across the *News Chronicle*, while David Meek's report in the *Manchester Evening News* read, 'Oh, how easy Madrid made goalscoring.' The *Daily Herald* ran with, 'Fabulous – Real Give Greatest Show On Earth', and the *Daily Mirror*, not content with one heading, used two – 'Real Perfection –That's What Did It,' and 'Battling Babes Hadn't A Chance'. It makes you wonder if the person who wrote the headline above Terence Elliott's report in the *Daily Express* had actually bothered to find out what the full-time score was when he penned 'Busby Boys Back To Life in Super Show'.

To win 6–1 you would probably imagine that the United defence had taken a hammering, as it had done the previous week when Preston North End blasted four past Harry Gregg without reply. The United 'keeper on that occasion, funnily enough, was the star man. But this time around the red shirts laboured manfully and restricted their visitors to a mere nine shots. Six from nine, however, is certainly a good average from the ghost-like figures appearing and disappearing at will beneath the glare of the floodlights.

United began the game well, prompted by Charlton and Quixall, although few expected them to gain the upper hand against Di Stefano and company, and they were soon proved right as the game was over as a contest by the 25th minute when Puskas scored his second.

The portly Hungarian opened the scoring in the seventh minute, appearing as if from nowhere to latch on to Didi's through ball and beat Gregg with ease. Puskas' second came eighteen minutes later, curling a left-footed shot past the United goalkeeper after Gento had done all the spade work.

Not to be outdone by his teammate, Di Stefano quickly took centre-stage, adding a third in the 32nd minute when he raced round Ronnie Cope before beating the helpless Gregg at a time when United were searching for a goal to put them right back into the game.

Four minutes prior to the interval it was 4–0. Canario's centre, following Gento's corner, was met by Di Stefano, with his back to goal, and he flicked it over his shoulder and into the net from close in.

There was little that Matt Busby could say to his mesmerised players at half-time, except to just keep plodding away. They should have reduced the leeway seconds after the restart when Albert Scanlon missed a golden opportunity, one that was actually harder to miss than score, but three minutes after the interval they did get the better of the Madrid defence when Bobby Charlton sent a 50-yard pass down the right. Warren Bradley took off from the halfway line and evaded a challenge from Lesmes before flashing the ball past Dominguez.

The goal was no more than United deserved, but it only accelerated Madrid back into gear and they rather painfully toyed with the United defence before scoring a fifth in the 63rd minute. A poor defensive clearance was pounced upon by Didi, the Brazilian pushing the ball through to Puskas, whose cross enabled the unmarked substitute Pepillo to score.

The scoring finally came to an end in the 78th minute when another defensive error saw the ball go directly to the feet of Gento, who wasted little time in blasting it directly back into the United net.

United's defensive fragility did rear its head once more, although credit had to be given to Foulkes for his sterling effort against Gento, reputed to be the best outside-left in the business. Had Cope managed a similar job against Di Stefano then who knows what might have happened. Both McGuinness and Goodwin did their best to keep Didi under close control.

At the opposite end of the pitch, the forwards certainly gave the Spaniards, who were on £50 per man to win this mere friendly but earned £80 due to the scoreline, plenty to think about. Quixall did his best to try and coax and cajole his teammates into life, but whenever there was a hint of danger a Madrid player was quickly in for the challenge. The United inside-forward missed a glorious opportunity when he shot over with the goal at his mercy. Two powerful drives from Bobby Charlton flashed past the Madrid goal with 'keeper Dominquez beaten, and his bad luck continued when the Madrid 'keeper managed to pull off two tremendous saves, leaving the United man standing with his head in his hands. Scanlon, on the other hand, was guilty of wasting several opportunities.

The scenes at full-time lived long in the memory of those present, as did the performance of the Spanish side, with the United support and team warmly applauding the Real Madrid players who stood, arms raised, in the centre circle. 'An ear-shattering ovation' is how Peter Slingsby in the *Manchester Evening Chronicle* described it, with the local scribe also quick to point out that he thought 'Madrid were never five goals better'.

For the armchair supporter the usual Thursday-night entertainment was bypassed as most of the second half was shown live, something of a rarity in those bygone days of black-and-white television.

Harry Gregg came in for some undeserved criticism following the game as he was spotted running from the pitch as soon as the final whistle blew. Many felt this was a show of poor sportsmanship due to his conceding of six goals, but it was simply due to the fact that he had to catch the night ferry to Ireland for an international fixture against Scotland in Belfast less than 48 hours later.

Despite their victory Real Madrid players and officials were warm in their praise for United. Emil Ostreicher, their team manager, was quick to single out Bobby Charlton as a player of vast potential, and it was clearly hinted that he would make an ideal replacement for any of Madrid's aging trio of superstars in Di Stefano, Puskas and Didi. Di Stefano was quick to admit after the game that 'the old United team were much better, but we must not forget that Mr Busby is still rebuilding.'

The United manager himself was not too concerned about the defeat and went as far as to say that he felt Albert Quixall compared favourably with both Puskas and Di Stefano but was certainly far better than Didi.

This fixture was the 'home' leg of a double-header, with United travelling to Madrid a few weeks later, but at the after-match dinner there was much conversation regarding making the fixtures an annual event. Fitting such fixtures into Madrid's heavy schedule would be the main problem in such games taking place on a regular basis.

United did travel to Spain on 11 November, although the game had originally been pencilled in for 21 October, and with something of an improved showing of form in the League they managed to compete with Madrid on a level that few would have imagined. Madrid once again scored six, but United, perhaps enjoying the comfort of the falling rain, managed five in reply.

In the 12th minute, Santamaria brought down Charlton, and Quixall scored from the spot after Dominguez had parried his first attempt. Two minutes later it was 2–0. Scanlon got the better of Marquitos and swung a long ball forward. Bradley raced past Pachin before sending a right-footed drive past the Madrid 'keeper with a little help of a deflection from Santamaria.

Harry Gregg made outstanding saves from Di Stefano and Mateos before the former pulled one back with a controversial penalty in the 21st minute. Di Stefano and Foulkes challenged for a bouncing ball just inside the area and it struck the United defender on the arm. The spot-kick rattled off the crossbar and into the net.

Numerous refereeing decisions went against United, but in the 33rd minute a four-man move between Goodwin, Charlton, Scanlon and Viollet, saw the latter score from five yards out to make it 3–1.

Gregg was again called upon to keep United in front, foiling Mateos on two occasions, but the Madrid number 10 finally got the better of the United 'keeper, sprinting away from a questionable offside position to score two minutes before the interval.

Bueno was put through by Di Stefano and scored the equaliser four minutes after the restart, and then the referee silenced the normally voracious Madrid crowd by awarding their favourites a penalty following a rather innocuous tackle by Goodwin on Mateos. What followed would never happen now, but clearly illustrates the direction that the game has gone. Di Stefano placed the ball on the spot, took a few steps back and then blasted the ball high over the bar in a deliberate act of sportsmanship.

Scanlon put Charlton through in the 56th minute to make it 4–2 and the impossible was back on, but it was not for long because Bueno hit United with a hat-trick, the goals coming in the 62nd, 76th and 80th minutes.

United, playing the same 11 that had conceded six at Old Trafford, kept plodding away and netted a fifth with two minutes remaining, substitute Dawson scoring with a low drive. The game finished with five for United against the best in Europe, but they still had to get the better of the Spaniards. That day would come.

Manchester United: Gregg, Foulkes, Carolan, Goodwin, Cope, McGuinness, Bradley, Quixall, Viollet, Charlton, Scanlon.
Scorer: Bradley.
Real Madrid: Dominguez, Marquitos, Lesmes, Vidal, Santamaria, Ruiz, Canario (substitute Pepillo), Didi, Di Stefano, Puskas, Gento.
Scorers: Puskas 2, Di Stefano 2, Pepillo, Gento.
Attendance: 63,500.

Team of the Decade

Ask any Manchester United supporter to name their 'team of the decade' from the 1950s and they would almost immediately start to reel off the names of those who made up Matt Busby's regular starting 11 between seasons 1955–56 and 1957–58, or at least the August to February period of the latter campaign.

Many, however, tend to forget that some of those who were an integral part of Matt Busby's first post-war trophy winning side, the FA Cup-winning team of 1948, also saw action in the early 1950s, with half a dozen of those FA Cup winners also lifting League Championship medals at the end of season 1951–52. One other failed to do so only because he had not reached the required number of appearances.

I had considered selecting the team in a 4–4–2 formation, but this, I then thought, would be completely alien to the line up of the period. Play often took on a different formation to the 1–2–3–5 that could be found in the match programmes, but I have decided to stick with this.

Who do we have to choose from and who will make the 1950s Team of the Decade? Perhaps it is best to start with a squad and then progress from there:

Goalkeepers:	Jack Crompton, Reg Allen, Ray Wood and Harry Gregg.
Full-backs:	Johnny Carey, John Aston, Roger Byrne and Bill Foulkes.
Half-backs:	Henry Cockburn, Eddie Colman, Duncan Edwards, Jackie Blanchflower, Mark Jones and Allenby Chilton.
Forwards:	Johnny Berry, Billy Whelan, Stan Pearson, Dennis Viollet, David Pegg, Tommy Taylor, Jack Rowley, Bobby Charlton and Albert Scanlon.

If we look at goalkeepers first, we immediately have something of a tough job.

Jack Crompton: Superb stopper of penalty-kicks, loyal and brave.

Reg Allen: League Championship winner in season 1951–52, but illness prevented him from achieving more within the game. Who knows what he may have achieved if he had been fit?

Ray Wood: An excellent shot stopper. The only goalkeeper to play in a Wembley Cup Final and not let in a goal, yet leave the field with a runners'-up medal. Did well enough to merit international recognition but still had his doubters who considered him rather suspect when it came to crosses.

Harry Gregg: Feared nothing and no one, and commanded his area as if his life depended upon it. Did not arrive at Old Trafford until 1958 so only saw action in the latter years of the decade.

As Jack Crompton, excellent as he was, made only made a handful of his 200-odd games for the club during the 1950s, I have decided against his inclusion for that reason alone. Reg Allen, despite his appearance record during this period being comparable to Gregg's, also fails to make the team as both Ray Wood and Harry Gregg were better goalkeepers.

So, the choice comes down to either Ray Wood or Harry Gregg for a place between the sticks, and after a great deal of thought I have decided to plump for **Harry Gregg**. As a man and a player, I have nothing but respect for Harry, and although he was more than unfortunate not to win anything while at United, while also overlapping into the 60s, I will give him the number-one jersey in this team of the decade, just edging out the man whom he replaced in the United line up.

The positions of right and left-back are by far the easiest to make, with there being no competition whatsoever against **Johnny Carey** and **Roger Byrne**. John Aston is also there for consideration, but even he would lift his hat to the pairing of Carey and Byrne, who would also challenge each other for the captain's armband.

Byrne's greatest asset was his speed, and few, if indeed any, wing-men got the better of him. Using his knowledge as a full-back enabled him to produce excellent displays at outside-left. He was a born leader who was not afraid to stand up to Matt Busby, but he still commanded the respect of his manager and fellow teammates.

Carey, like Byrne, could play anywhere, and he did, with even a game in goal to his credit. There were few, if any, better full-backs within the game at this time and Carey would, again like Byrne, be a candidate for an all-time United 11, never mind one from the 1950s.

We now require three half-backs, or actually two as there is one name that would be shouted out as soon as anyone announced that they were selecting a team from the 1950s, or, for that matter, an all-time great Manchester United side. Nothing more can be written about **Duncan Edwards**, so I will not make any attempt to do so, other than to say that the number-six jersey is his.

The centre-half position has two candidates in Allenby Chilton and Mark Jones. Both were no-nonsense defenders who would have provided a solid backbone to the team, but, for his strength and almost ever-present appearance record, the next name on the team sheet is that of **Allenby Chilton**. He was one of the game's real hard men at a time when there were many and was the only ever present in the 1951–52 Championship side, a player that you could certainly rely upon when the going got tough.

Completing the half-back line I have gone for a more defensive type of player, which would have enabled Duncan to enjoy more freedom in his role. I could have, and certainly did, consider giving the number-four shirt to the diminutive but highly effective and influential Eddie Colman, but in the end I have gone for **Jackie Blanchflower**. The totally versatile Irishman would have complemented Chilton, and if the defence did take on something of a back four look then Blanchflower would have given the partnership something of a Ferdinand/Vidic air.

Selecting the forward line is not really too much of a problem, as many of the positions simply pick themselves due to the longevity of those who find their way into the 'squad'. At number seven I have selected **Johnny Berry**, but, to be honest, there was no one else to consider really, because the former Birmingham City player made the outside-right spot his own between September 1951 and February 1958, missing few games as he helped United to three League Championships.

Playing alongside Berry, I have gone for a player who only came into the side on a regular basis during season 1956–57, but his ability was well known around Old Trafford from his initial appearances in the United Youth side. **Liam Whelan** had more strings to his bow than just the silky skills that so impressed the Brazilian national side who witnessed a United youth-team performance during a Blue Stars tournament in Switzerland. He was also a noted goal scorer and it is his added ability to find the back of the net that earns him his place in this line up.

Leading the front line creates a debate between Jack Rowley or Tommy Taylor, with both individuals being noted goalscorers. I decided to play safe and seek the opinion of my friend, Tom Clare, who watched United during those halcyon days. In Tom's eye there was 'no contest this selection. I just wish that youngsters today could have seen this fellow play. In the modern day, younger United fans eulogise about van Nistelrooy, but, for me, Taylor was by far the better all-round player, and had he been around today scoring records would be gone for a Burton! Lethal in the air, and I have still yet to see a better or harder header of the ball. Tommy was lightning quick, with two very good feet and an understanding with Dennis Viollet that was almost telepathic. He would drag defenders all over the place, making acres of space for other players to do damage. When you look at his goalscoring record for United, you have to also remember that he never took any penalty-kicks!' **Tommy Taylor** claims the number-nine shirt.

Partnering the lad from Barnsley, I have gone for yet another individual with an eye for goal in **Dennis Viollet**, and, like Tom Clare said, the one-time City supporter had a very good understanding with Tommy Taylor as well as an excellent scoring record. Stan Pearson also came into the reckoning, but in the end I decided to give the nod to Viollet.

There is only one shirt to fill and that is the number 11. In order to add the final player to this team I am going to bypass the undoubted skill of David Pegg, while also pushing Albert Scanlon to the side, and I will make a similar selection choice to that of Matt Busby, selecting **Jack Rowley** ahead of the more orthodox wide men. Busby saw the additional benefits of playing Rowley out on the wing, so I will do likewise and hope that the 'goals for' would by far out weight the 'goals against'.

So, that is it. There is no place in the line up for the likes of Eddie Colman, Bobby Charlton or Bill Foulkes, but the latter two will have the opportunity to stake their claim in the 1960s team of the decade. Colman, however, would undoubtedly get a place on the bench.

No doubt some, many or most of you might disagree with the selection, but, like everything, it is simply a matter of personal choice, and therefore I have selected this Manchester United team of the decade for the 1950s:

Gregg, Carey, Byrne, Blanchflower, Chilton, Edwards, Berry, Whelan, Taylor, Viollet and Rowley.